'There is something deli[...] his A-game, and that's what we get with [...] *Muslims and Christians Worship the Same God?* Few topics are more important in today's world, and few authors are more qualified to address it. Thank you, Andy, for giving us this excellent and important book!'

Bruxy Cavey, Pastor, The Meeting House, and author of *The End of Religion*

'A nuanced and sensitive examination, from an overtly Christian perspective, of how to negotiate a truth that is no less self-evident for being one that many prefer to draw a veil across: Christianity and Islam are not remotely the same.'

Tom Holland, author of *Dominion* and *In the Shadow of the Sword*

'*Do Christians and Muslims Worship the Same God?* is a must-read in today's culture of religious diversity. You will appreciate his deep understanding of both Islam and Christianity, as well as the British humour interjected into this crucial conversation. Muslims and Christians no longer live in separate communities but, rather, interact on a daily basis in schools and work settings. This book is a great resource to foster healthy dialogue and understanding.'

Fouad Masri, President/CEO, Crescent Project

'We hear the question often: do Christians and Muslims worship the same God? Many in our pluralistic world want the answer to be a resounding "Yes", but few are actually qualified to answer that question. We need thinkers who have studied both religions extensively. Andy Bannister is just such an expert and he helps us to wrestle with this important question with the depth and care it deserves.'

Randy Newman, Senior Fellow at The C. S. Lewis Institute and author of *Questioning Evangelism*

'With warmth, wit and approachability, Dr Andy Bannister has drawn on his extensive knowledge of Islam and Christianity to bring us a book of real wisdom. He gets right to the heart of the questions and offers the reader accessible evidence to consider the essential claims of two faiths. I highly recommend this readable yet thoroughly researched book as a must-read for the curious, whether you have faith already or not. Prepare to be entertained, edified and gripped – I found myself unable to put it down.'
Dr Amy Orr-Ewing, President, OCCA The Oxford Centre for Christian Apologetics

'In his latest book, Andy Bannister tackles one of the most challenging questions of Christian–Muslim dialogue. His arguments are lucid and his conclusions compelling. At the same time, he writes with respect, grace and humour. This book is a must-read for all interested in inter-religious issues, both believers and non-believers.'
Peter G. Riddell, SOAS University of London and Australian College of Theology

'Andy Bannister's profound grasp of both Islam and Christianity make this book a unique and accessible resource for an important debate taking place in our churches and wider communities. Andy's good humour and capable scholarship bring clarity to a notoriously difficult yet increasingly significant discussion. He is persistently challenging, consistently provoking, deeply searching and endlessly witty! This book is for all who are concerned to think carefully about what it means to hold Christian beliefs faithfully in our contemporary multi-religious context.'
Anna Robbins, President and Dean of Theology, Acadia University

'*Do Muslims and Christians Worship the Same God?* is a sharp-witted, big-hearted and clear-minded romp through one of the most pressing religious questions of our time. You will laugh your way through some of the key differences between Islamic and Christian belief, discovering just why they matter so much for humanity. This is classic Bannister and essential reading for those seeking both intellectual clarity and relational generosity in Christian–Muslim relations.'

Dr Richard Shumack, Research Fellow, Centre for Public Christianity, and Director, Arthur Jeffery Centre for the Study of Islam, Melbourne School of Theology

Andy Bannister is the Director of Solas, an Adjunct Research Fellow at the Arthur Jeffery Centre for the Study of Islam at Melbourne School of Theology and an Adjunct Faculty member at Wycliffe College, University of Toronto. Unusual in being a Christian academic and public speaker with a PhD in Islamic Studies, Andy frequently speaks and teaches throughout the UK, Europe, Canada and the USA. He regularly addresses audiences of all faiths (and none) on issues relating to faith, culture and society.

Andy is the author of several books, including *An Oral-Formulaic Study of the Qur'an* (2014), *Heroes: Five leaders from whose lives we can learn* (2015) and *The Atheist Who Didn't Exist: Or: the dreadful consequences of bad arguments* (2015). He has also contributed to the multi-author volume *Healthy Faith and the Coronavirus Crisis: Thriving in the COVID-19 pandemic* (2020).

When not travelling, speaking or writing, Andy lives in Scotland with his wife Astrid and their two children, Caitriona and Christopher. He is an avid mountaineer and is busy climbing his way through the Scottish Munros. Andy can be found on social media at <@andygbannister>.

DO MUSLIMS AND CHRISTIANS WORSHIP THE SAME GOD?

Dear Priscilla,

Thanks for your support
for Solas — enjoy the
book!

Andy Bannister

DO MUSLIMS AND CHRISTIANS WORSHIP THE SAME GOD?

Andy Bannister

INTER-VARSITY PRESS
36 Causton Street, London SW1P 4ST, England
Email: ivp@ivpbooks.com
Website: www.ivpbooks.com

First published 2021

British Library Cataloguing-in-Publication Data
A catalogue record for this book is available from the British Library.

ISBN: 978–1–78974–229–9
eBook ISBN: 978–1–78974–230–5

Set in Minion Pro 10.25/13.75pt
Typeset in Great Britain by CRB Associates, Potterhanworth, Lincolnshire
Printed in Great Britain by Ashford Colour Press Ltd, Gosport, Hampshire

Produced on paper from sustainable forests

*Inter-Varsity Press publishes Christian books that are true to the Bible and that
communicate the gospel, develop discipleship and strengthen the church for its mission
in the world.*

*IVP originated within the Inter-Varsity Fellowship, now the Universities and Colleges
Christian Fellowship, a student movement connecting Christian Unions in universities and
colleges throughout Great Britain, and a member movement of the International Fellowship
of Evangelical Students. Website: www.uccf.org.uk. That historic association is maintained,
and all senior IVP staff and committee members subscribe to the UCCF Basis of Faith.*

In memoriam

Nabeel Qureshi (1983–2017)
Keith Small (1959–2018)
Jamie Roth (1969–2020)

Thank you, each one of you, for your friendship
and your encouragement. You are all sorely missed.

There are a dozen views about everything until you know
the answer. Then there's never more than one.
(C. S. Lewis)

Truth stands out clearly from error.
(The Qur'an)

Then you will know the truth, and the truth will set you free.
(Jesus Christ)

Contents

Note to the reader   xii

1   Baptists, beards and burqas
    Common assumptions about religion   1

2   The elephant in the room
    Why it's not arrogant to say that someone's religion isn't true   15

3   Life, the universe and everything
    Four questions for comparing and contrasting beliefs   34

4   Will the real God please stand up?
    Comparing the Bible's and the Qur'an's views of God   44

5   How much more than dust?
    The Bible, the Qur'an and what it means to be human   72

6   The crack in everything
    What in the world is wrong with the world?   89

7   Self-help or salvation?
    The Qur'an, the Bible and the cure for all that ails us   107

8   The misfit Messiah
    How putting Jesus in his place helps us see God clearly   132

9   For the love of God, come home
    Why Christianity is the most inclusive exclusive faith
    in the world   156

Further reading   181

Acknowledgments   185

Note to the reader

Throughout the book, quotations from the Qur'an are taken from various translations, including Arthur J. Arberry, *The Koran Interpreted: A translation* (London: George Allen & Unwin, 1955), Arthur J. Droge, *The Qur'ān: A new annotated translation* (Sheffield: Equinox, 2013), Marmaduke Pickthall, *The Meaning of the Glorious Koran* (London: Everyman's Library, 1992 [1930]) and Abdullah Yusuf Ali, *The Holy Qur'ān* (Birmingham: IPCI, 1999 [1937]).

Quotations from the hadith are taken from the digital editions at <www.sunnah.com>.

Also, throughout the book, the word 'god' is found spelt both with a lower-case and an upper-case initial letter (that is, 'god' and 'God'). That's not a mistake nor sloppiness by the author, but quite deliberate. Where the word refers to a *specific* god (such as 'the God of the Bible' or 'the God of the Qur'an'), then a capital 'G' is used, as the word is clearly a title. Otherwise, a lower-case 'g' is used (as in 'the concept of god' or 'the gods of the ancient world'), as it's simply functioning as a humble noun.

All vowels used in this book were obtained from sustainable sources.

1

Baptists, beards and burqas
Common assumptions about religion

I was brought up in a very multicultural and multireligious part of south London. Where I lived, you could choose from a thousand and one different belief systems: from Buddhism to Judaism, Hinduism to Sikhism, Jainism to humanism, and more. You could even be a Wimbledon Football Club fan; we called that masoch*ism*. Within a mile or two of my home, there were Christian churches, a Sikh gurdwara and a couple of mosques. Had they found the funds, the Jedis would no doubt have set up a temple somewhere in the neighbourhood.[1]

As I grew up, religion was *everywhere* and, despite the predictions of many secularists that it would go the way of vinyl records and flared trousers, four decades on from my childhood, religion is still everywhere.

And it's *growing*.

According to the latest research from the well-respected Pew Research Center, by 2060 Christianity will have grown to 32% of the world's population, Islam to 31%,[2] and the number of people identifying as atheists or agnostics will have declined to 12.5%.[3]

---

1 In recent decades, every time a national census has been taken, many Brits have enjoyed writing things like 'Jedi' in answer to the 'What religion are you?' question. They're clearly a force to be reckoned with.

2 See 'Projected change in global population, 2015–2060', Pew Research Center, 31 March 2017, <www.pewforum.org/2017/04/05/the-changing-global-religious-landscape/pf_17-04-05_projectionsupdate_changepopulation640px>.

3 See 'Size and projected growth of major religious groups, 2015–2060', Pew Research Center, 3 April 2017, <www.pewforum.org/2017/04/05/the-changing-global-religious-landscape/pf-04-05-2017_-projectionsupdate-00-07>.

Those are the global statistics. But zoom in and you discover religion has not vanished here in the West either, no matter what some overly excitable journalists may claim. While some older, established churches have shrunk, more popular forms of Christianity have sprung up, often invigorated by immigration, which has brought lively forms of the faith from Africa, Asia and Latin America. Immigration has also imported a thousand and one entirely different religions to the West, everything from animism to Zoroastrianism – a literal A-to-Z of belief systems, all jostling for attention in the religious marketplace. Among these newcomers, particular attention has been focused on Islam, with over 30 million Muslims now living and worshipping in Europe and North America.[4]

Even among secular-minded Westerners, often tempted to view religion with suspicion while trying to pretend they're far too sophisticated for such things, religion has simply morphed into other forms. 'Spirituality', for example.

I lived for some years in Canada. Shortly after emigrating to what friends had told me was a very secular country, I took a short flight from Vancouver to Vancouver Island on a tiny plane that bounced around the sky like a ping-pong ball in a tumble dryer. To distract myself from thinking about unhelpful things like metal fatigue and terminal velocity, I pulled out the in-flight magazine, a glossy little production of about a dozen pages. Six of those pages were given over to an article on ghosts – how to know if your house has one, how to befriend it, how to ensure it brings positive vibes to your life and so on.

Later, waiting to catch the return flight back to Vancouver, I got chatting to a man at an airport coffee stand who told me that he was off to attend a conference to help him discover his inner divinity.

---

4   See 'Europe's growing Muslim population', Pew Research Center, 29 November 2017, <www.pewforum.org/2017/11/29/europes-growing-muslim-population>; and 'New estimates show U.S. Muslim population continues to grow', Pew Research Center, 3 January 2018, <www.pewresearch.org/fact-tank/2018/01/03/new-estimates-show-u-s-muslim-population-continues-to-grow>.

'I am God,' he announced, 'and so are you. By the way, do you know where the washroom is?'

All of this in *secular* Canada. In other Western countries, even atheists have got in on the spirituality act, publishing books on topics like how to find 'spirituality without religion'.[5]

Given that religion is everywhere and growing, perhaps the biggest question facing us is: how can we live together despite our differences? How do we all get along? A very common answer is: let's affirm that it doesn't matter what you believe as long as you're sincere. If Christianity works for you, that's great; but if Islam floats your boat, then go for it. After all, aren't all religions *essentially* the same?

That was certainly my assumption growing up in south London. I belonged to a Christian family; every week we attended the local Baptist church and, as a teenager, I enjoyed youth group, Bible studies and, with my friends, working out ways to pass the time during boring sermons, such as rolling marbles beneath the pews and seeing who could get theirs closest to the front of the church without getting caught.

While on the weekends most of the friends I hung out with were Christians, at school it was an entirely different matter. The high school I attended was full of many different nationalities, especially from the Indian subcontinent, and many of my classmates were Muslims. (London's first Muslim mayor, Sadiq Khan, went to the same school as me. If only I'd had the foresight to get his autograph before he became famous.)

Some of my closest friends at school were Muslims, including my friend Ahmad who, like me, was an avid member of the school chess club; he and I had both made the same very practical discovery that joining the chess club got you out of playing rugby in the rain.

---

5 Just two of many examples: Sam Harris, *Waking Up: Searching for spirituality without religion* (London: Transworld, 2014); Alain de Botton, *Religion for Atheists: A non-believer's guide to the uses of religion* (London: Penguin, 2013).

I was a Christian, Ahmad was a Muslim, but we didn't talk about religion. I think we just saw each other as 'religious', whatever that meant.

As a teenager, I never really spent any time at all wondering what my Muslim classmates and friends *actually* believed. If you'd asked me, I think I would probably have assumed it was broadly similar to what I believed. After all, I went to church, they went to mosque; I read the Bible, they read the Qur'an; I believed in Jesus, they believed in Muhammad. And all of us got the mickey taken out of us by the atheists in the class (a small but noisily vocal minority) who liked to call all of us, Christians and Muslims alike, 'religious nutters'.

So it seemed to me that we were all worshipping the same god, in some vague not-quite-sure-how-it-all-fits-together kind of way. In my mind, Muslims were just like Baptists, only with beards and burqas.

Assuming similarity

The idea that Muslims and Christians are essentially the same is still doing the rounds today. My naive teenage assumptions have gone mainstream. In particular, one frequently hears people lump together the three major monotheistic religions of Judaism, Christianity and Islam under the general term 'Abrahamic faiths'. To many people it seems obvious. Muslims, Christians and Jews all believe in one god, they all believe in scripture, they all believe in heaven, indeed they even have figures like Abraham in common,[6] so surely it's clear that these three religious traditions are branches of the same tree, cousins in the same family. For example, Anglican vicar and journalist Giles Fraser wrote: 'Christians should remind themselves that Muslims

---

6 As well as appearing in the Bible, in both the Old Testament (the part of the Bible also sacred to Jews) and the New Testament, Abraham is frequently mentioned in the Qur'an, with an Arabized form of his name (Ibrahim).

are our brothers and sisters with whom we share a faith in the living God.'[7] While across the Atlantic, in the run-up to the 2020 US presidential election, Joe Biden cheerfully announced: 'I wish we taught more in our schools about the Islamic faith . . . [What people] don't realize is that we all come from the same root here in terms of our fundamental, basic beliefs.'[8]

This is not just a popular assumption; one can also find it being expressed by serious-minded scholars. Miroslav Volf, an incredibly highly regarded Christian theologian based at Yale University, wrote a popular book addressing this whole question of the relationship between Christianity and Islam. In the opening pages of *Allah: A Christian response*, Volf writes: 'Christians and Muslims worship one and the same God. They understand God's character partly differently, but the object of their worship is the same. I reject the idea that Muslims worship a different God than do Jews and Christians.'[9] The leader of the Roman Catholic Church, Pope Francis, during a trip to Morocco in 2019, also leapt on the hey-isn't-it-great-we-believe-in-the-same-god bandwagon, choosing to pontificate in, of all things, a tweet: 'We Christians and Muslims believe in God, the Creator and the Merciful, who created people to live like brothers and sisters, respecting each other in their diversity, and helping one another in their needs.'[10] To be fair, Pope Francis wasn't entirely innovating here, but reflecting a theme that goes back some sixty years to the Second Vatican Council, which stated that Muslims 'together with us adore the one, merciful God'.[11]

7 Giles Fraser, 'The Hagia Sophia is for prayer, not pictures', *UnHerd*, 10 July 2020, <www.unherd.com/thepost/the-hagia-sophia-is-for-prayer-not-pictures>.

8 'Joe Biden speech at the Million Muslim Votes Summit transcript July 2020', *Rev*, 20 July 2020, <www.rev.com/blog/transcripts/joe-biden-speech-at-the-million-muslim-votes-summit-transcript-july-20>.

9 Miroslav Volf, *Allah: A Christian response* (New York: HarperOne, 2011), p. 14.

10 Pope Francis, @Pontifex Twitter account, 29 March 2019, <www.twitter.com/pontifex/status/1111697027107184640>.

11 Pope John Paul VI, *Lumen Gentium*, II.16, 21 November 1964, <www.vatican.va/archive/hist_councils/ii_vatican_council/documents/vat-ii_const_19641121_lumen-gentium_en.html>.

A fascinating survey in 2018 of British and American Christians revealed how versions of this idea are seeping down from the lofty world of theologians, vicars and popes into the wider church. The market research company ComRes surveyed thousands of Christians about their beliefs and, as part of their survey, asked respondents whether they would agree with the statement 'God accepts the worship of all religions, including Christianity, Judaism, and Islam'; 63% of British Christians and 80% of American Christians said that they would.[12] While this may be a watered-down version of the full-fat, super-sized 'same god' idea, nevertheless, it's still very much in the same ballpark and is one more indicator of how the assumption that religions in general (and Christianity and Islam in particular) are essentially the same (at least in most of the important ways) is becoming ever more mainstream.

Putting assumptions to the test

The problem with assumptions is precisely that: *they're assumptions.* Whether it's a mildly innocuous one, like the assumption that the humble tomato is a vegetable (it's not, it's a fruit, although pointing that out still hasn't made my five-year-old willing to eat one), or a piece of folk medical advice, like 'Don't swim within an hour of eating or you'll get cramp' (not true; besides, if it's the British seaside you're swimming at, you'll freeze to death long before you get cramp), or my soon-corrected assumption that 'when you get married you can carry on all your bachelor domestic habits and your wife won't complain' (that one survived less than a month), the thing about

---

12 You can explore the whole survey at <www.thestateoftheology.com/uk> (for the UK results) or <https://thestateoftheology.com> (for the USA results). And by way of illustration, see the letter in the *Church Times* of 24 July 2020 by Paul Reynolds, which casually remarks that 'the God whom Muslims worship is the same God as we worship': <www.churchtimes.co.uk/articles/2020/24-july/comment/letters-to-the-editor/letters-to-the-editor>.

assumptions is that it often isn't until we *put them to the test* that we discover they don't hold up.

My own assumption that Christianity and Islam were broadly the same survived my school years and lasted until the late 1990s. Then one weekend, a visiting speaker came to our church and gave a seminar on how, as Christians, we should engage with our Muslim friends and neighbours. This was the first time that I'd ever really heard anything taught in a systematic way about what Muslims believed. Of course, I'd sat through the mandatory Religious Studies lessons at school, but those had been pretty cursory and about as exciting as a wet weekend in Milton Keynes.

But this speaker was very different. Jay was lively and dynamic and, over several hours, gave a fascinating overview of Islamic beliefs and history, as well as sharing some of the new discoveries scholars and academics were making about the Qur'an and the origins of Islam that challenged the traditional story of how the religion began.

Then Jay explained how, every Sunday afternoon, he was taking groups of Christians to Speakers' Corner to dialogue, debate and talk about Christianity with the many Muslims to be found there. Speakers' Corner is part of Hyde Park in London and since the mid-nineteenth century has become affectionately known as the world centre of free speech. At Speakers' Corner, no matter who you are, you can stand on a ladder or a soapbox and talk about *anything* – politics, philosophy, religion, sport – and, if you're informed, witty or entertaining, you can draw a crowd. Jay had discovered that Speakers' Corner was a great place for Christians to meet and debate with Muslims.

I'd never heard of anything like this before in my life. The Christian tradition I'd been brought up in was fairly quietist. Christians, in my experience, stood on the sidelines, usually dressed in bad knitwear, and politely raised their hands when they wanted to speak or coughed until somebody noticed them and asked their opinion or offered them a throat sweet. But Christians standing on ladders, talking publicly about what they believed, debating Muslims, getting heckled . . . It sounded incredible, it sounded amazing, it sounded frankly terrifying.

'Oh, it's *easy*,' said Jay, when I chatted to him over the lunch break. 'Why don't you come to Speakers' Corner next week and see what we do?'

So the next weekend I found myself standing outside Marble Arch London Underground station, on a soggy Sunday afternoon, not quite sure what I was doing there. A tap on my shoulder startled me and I turned round to see Jay, carrying two stepladders, one slung over each shoulder.

'Why have you got two stepladders?' I asked.

'One for me, one for you,' he replied nonchalantly.

'I thought you said I should come to *see* what you do.'

'Well, the best view of Speakers' Corner is from the top of a ladder. Besides, everyone should try street preaching.'

'But I've never "preached" on the street.'

'It's *easy*. Now come along – the Muslims are waiting.'

'But I've never debated with a Muslim before.'

'That's easy too.'

And so it was I found myself, twenty minutes later, balanced atop a wobbly stepladder, surrounded by a crowd of a couple of hundred Muslims, giving a very public demonstration of the fact that just because a large, enthusiastic, bearded American extrovert says something is 'easy', it isn't necessarily so.

To say that my first attempt at street preaching went 'badly' is to flirt wildly with understatement, on a par with describing Mount Everest as 'bigger than a duck'. While it's true, it probably misses something fairly fundamental. Jay had suggested that I try speaking about something simple, for example, tackling the topic 'Why I'm a Christian'. And so I rambled on for a couple of minutes in a feeble voice, barely making myself heard above the rain and the traffic rumbling past on nearby Park Lane.

The crowd stared in polite bemusement until I eventually dried up.

Jay decided to try to help me out by prompting me with a few questions. He was an old pro and had a voice like a foghorn, so the crowds began to wake up again, but I just froze with fear.

So far, so awful, but then the heckling began.

'Look at the Christian – he has nothing to say!'

'He has nothing to say because the Bible has no answers!'

'That Christian needs the Qur'an!'

'Islam is the answer!'

'*Allahu akbar!*'

Feeling that this was one horrible mistake, I stepped down from the ladder, thinking it best to leave public speaking to the experts, and was promptly surrounded by a throng of Muslims who had a barrage of questions ready for me. 'Hasn't the Bible been corrupted and only the Qur'an perfectly preserved?' asked one man and, before I could think what to say, another piped up with 'Why do you Christians blaspheme by worshipping Jesus (peace be upon him) who was just a prophet of Allah?' I turned to face this new questioner when somebody from behind shouted, 'You Christians say you believe in one God but talk about the Father, the Son and the Holy Spirit. Yet one plus one plus one equals three, not one!' Occasional cries of '*Allahu akbar!*' would drift up from the crowd whenever somebody lobbed what the others thought was a particularly tricky theological zinger. I had answers to *none* of them. So much for Christianity and Islam being broadly the same! My new Muslim friends were very clear that the two religions were *wildly* different; only one of them was right, and that was self-evidently Islam.

'Well,' said Jay, stroking his beard thoughtfully as we debriefed later over a coffee. 'That didn't go too badly for your first time, all things considered.'

'Not *too* badly?' I muttered, drowning my sorrows with a swig of caffeine.

'Oh, sure. The last newbie I had on the ladder was so traumatized, he never came back. Moved to Canada in the end, I think.'

Looking for the evidence

On the train home I reflected a lot about what had happened at Speakers' Corner. About how when I had the chance to talk about my Christian faith, I had nothing to say. And how when my new Muslim friends had asked questions, I had no answers. But they seemed to know everything about what they believed, and had a hundred and one reasons why they thought Islam was true, why they thought Christianity was false and why they believed I should become a Muslim.

I thought about this all the way home and all through the evening, and later I lay awake in bed, still chewing things over. Were there *no* good reasons to be a Christian? Did the Muslims have better answers because Islam was *true*? I stared restlessly up into the darkness of the bedroom as I pondered these troubling questions until, finally, about 3 a.m., my wife, whose patience knows almost no bounds, poked me in the ribs and asked why I was tossing and turning and keeping us both awake. I explained what I was struggling to process and her wise words were: 'Maybe you should read a book or something – ideally in the morning.'

Deciding this was a good plan, the following morning I caught the bus into town and paid a visit to the local bookshop, which was one of those delightfully old-fashioned establishments packed to bursting point with rambling miles of endless wooden shelves, creaking under the weight of books of every possible size and shape. I explained my predicament to the man behind the counter, who peered thoughtfully over his glasses at me.

'Young man,' he said kindly, 'you need apologetics.'

'Apolo-what-ix?' I asked. I thought it sounded like some kind of breakfast cereal.

'Apo-lo-getics,' he repeated. 'It's the part of theology concerned with giving reasons and evidence for the Christian faith. You'll find it down there.' He pointed down an aisle. 'Turn left at epistemology, first right at eschatology and then straight on past hermeneutics.'

Rather than ask who Herman was, why he was drunk and why he was into escapology, I scurried off among the shelves and returned a while later with a small pile of books that had caught my eye, all of which, in various ways, promised to equip me with answers to big questions about the Christian faith or enable me to better understand what my Muslim friends believed and ask them probing questions too.[13]

For the next few weeks I read voraciously, regularly revisiting the bookshop to purchase more, and when, a month later, I returned for a second visit to Speakers' Corner I was feeling decidedly more chipper. I was well read, I felt prepared, I felt confident, I was ready with answers to all the questions and challenges my Muslim friends had asked the last time. What could possibly go wrong?

They had *new* questions.

Lots of new questions.

Once again, I was surrounded by a throng of Muslims eager to overpower a Christian with objections, difficulties and dozens of reasons why they thought that, far from Islam and Christian being similar, Islam was *superior*.

Thus, the following day it was back to the bookshop, left at epistemology, right at eschatology and straight on past hermeneutics, to return with another pile of reading.

But for all the hard mental effort of thinking, investigating and really working out what I believed and why, this was actually fun. And so it became my routine for the next six months. Speakers'

---

13 I still have three of those first purchases on my shelves: Josh McDowell, *Evidence That Demands a Verdict* (London: Thomas Nelson, 1979); C. S. Lewis, *Mere Christianity* (Glasgow: Collins, 1990); Norman Geisler and Abdu Saleeb, *Answering Islam: The crescent in the light of the cross* (Grand Rapids, MI: Baker, 1993).

Corner on Sunday afternoons, reading during the week and occasional comments from my wife as to whether a different hobby – stamp collecting, competitive cheese-making or lion taming – might be easier.

Those six months of hard graft, of having my Christian faith challenged at Speakers' Corner, of being forced to read deeply to find out if what I believed was true – and to investigate the foundations of what my Muslim friends believed – all the reading, conversations and debates slowly began to do something to me. They gave me a passion for talking publicly about what I believed and learning to defend it; they kindled a love of learning (I hadn't been to university at this point – I wasn't from a university-attending kind of family); and they stirred in me a love for Muslims. I loved their questions, I admired their passion for what they believed and I enjoyed their willingness to talk about it boldly without apology.

All of this excited me so much that I clearly needed to pursue it further. Before long, I had applied for a three-year degree course in Philosophy and Theology. That degree eventually led to doctoral studies and, to cut a long and winding story short, I found myself, some years later, at the end of my academic journey with less hair, a large overdraft and a PhD in Islamic Studies, my thesis focusing on the way that the oral environment of seventh-century Arabia had left its mark on the text of the Qur'an.[14] When I went into full-time study I had promised my wife, 'This will only take three years.' It had taken eleven.

Over those eleven years, I studied Christianity and Islam in tremendous detail. I had to learn the languages of the Bible and the Qur'an and study the original texts. I dived deep into the origins of the two faiths and looked at their histories. I immersed myself in the biographies of their founders: Jesus in the case of Christianity, Muhammad in the case of Islam.

---

14 My thesis was published as *An Oral-Formulaic Study of the Qur'an* (New York: Lexington Books, 2014).

The more I studied Christianity and Islam at the highest academic level, the more I was drawn, inexorably, to two conclusions. First, there were *major* differences between the two religions. Far from being broadly the same with superficial differences, Islam and Christianity were fundamentally different, with mere cosmetic similarities. My old idea that they were all but identical had been based on ignorance. Just as somebody who says, 'Every book in the library is essentially the same – it's only booksellers out for a quick profit who tell you differently' isn't displaying wisdom but exposing a startling lack of reading, so the person, like my younger self, who opines that Christianity and Islam are more or less the same probably hasn't taken the time to study them in detail. Once you do, the differences become ever more apparent.

More than that, the more deeply I studied them, the more I put in the long hours of forensically examining Islam and Christianity, especially looking at the *evidence* for the claims made by these two faiths, the more I came to the conclusion that Christianity was true, that there were excellent reasons to believe the Bible, that the claims of Jesus could be put rigorously to the test and they stood up.

After eleven years of painstakingly examining the evidence, I had come to the firm conclusion that Christianity was true – uniquely, exclusively true – and Islam was not merely wholly different, but also *false*. The claims of Jesus bore the weight of careful scrutiny, while the claims of Muhammad did not.

Now, to some people's ears, words as bold as these will sound incredibly arrogant and breathtakingly narrow-minded. We live in an age where people are very nervous of exclusive claims about truth. So, in the next chapter let's address the elephant in the room: whether it is a problem to say, 'My religious beliefs are true and yours are false.'

Key takeaways

- Religion is growing, both globally and in the West. Far from ours being a secular age, it is an increasingly religious age. This means that one of the greatest questions facing us in the twenty-first century is: how can we all live together despite our deep differences in beliefs?

- The idea that Muslims and Christians worship the same god, that Christianity and Islam are (along with Judaism) part of a great tribe of 'Abrahamic faiths', is widespread, at both academic and popular levels.

- The assumption that 'all religions are essentially the same' is usually held by people who haven't studied any of them properly. Once you begin studying and comparing any of the world's major faith traditions more deeply, the differences quickly become apparent.

2

The elephant in the room

Why it's not arrogant to say that someone's religion isn't true

The elephant was not impressed. Earlier that morning it had been standing under the shade of a banyan tree, minding its own business while chewing thoughtfully through a pile of leaves. Suddenly the gate to its enclosure had been thrown open and a bunch of excited men had rushed in and begun poking at it with sticks. Amid much shouting and gesturing, the elephant had found itself driven towards the rear doors of the palace, then down a long corridor, before finally emerging in a large throne room.

On a raised platform at one end of the room sat an impressively robed king on an equally impressive throne. Either side of him stood a collection of courtiers, nobles and miscellaneous officials. The elephant plodded wearily into the centre of the throne room, an expression of bemused patience on its face. One of the courtiers rose to his feet and cried out in a loud voice, 'Bring in the blind men!'

A small doorway on the far side of the room was flung dramatically open, the effect only slightly ruined by its bouncing off the wall and rebounding shut again, to a very audible 'Ouch!' from the other side. It opened again, more cautiously this time, and four elderly men, clad in identical grey robes and each waving a white stick in front of him, entered the room.

The courtier cried out for a second time: 'Gentlemen! In the room before you stands a beast the like of which you have never before

15

encountered, the mighty elephant! His Royal Majesty would have you encounter the creature and then describe to us what you conclude an elephant is like. There is a prize of ten thousand rupees for the closest correct answer!'

A hush fell on the room. The elephant munched its leaves thoughtfully as the first blind man took tentative steps forward, hands waving in front of him. As he approached the front of the elephant, the first part of the creature his hands encountered was its trunk. He gave it a thoughtful tug and then kneaded it experimentally, like a gastronome assessing a sausage.

'Your Majesty,' he announced confidently, 'an elephant is like a python!'

A small round of applause broke out, at which point the elephant took the opportunity to trumpet loudly, causing everybody in the room to jump.

Next it was the turn of the second blind man to shuffle forward. Again, arms waving before him, he approached the elephant and soon stumbled into the side of the beast. Feeling his way around, like a mime artist describing an invisible box, the blind man explored for a moment before announcing, 'Your Majesty, my friend is wrong! An elephant is like a wall.'

Once more there was polite applause. Meanwhile, the elephant, increasingly bored and wondering when all this nonsense would end, shuffled nonchalantly sideways and knocked the second blind man off his feet.

The third blind man now advanced towards the centre of the room. One step, two steps, three steps and then . . . What was that? Stretching his arms wide, he hugged one of the elephant's legs. Ah, it was obvious, wasn't it?

'Oh King!' he cried out. 'I have no idea what my two friends have been smoking, for surely an elephant is like a tree!'

He beamed with delight at the ensuing applause but then quickly yelped in agony, as the elephant took a step forward and stood, with all the care and gentleness that only a creature weighing several tons can deploy, firmly on his foot.[1]

Finally, it was the fourth blind man's turn. He advanced on the elephant cautiously, having just heard the cry of pain of his compatriot. Circling as he got nearer, he ended up approaching the beast from the rear, where his waving hands caught hold of the elephant's tail. He gave it an enthusiastic tug and beamed with delight.

'Your Majesty,' he called out triumphantly, 'my friends are all wrong. For it is obvious an elephant is like a rope!'

Again, a smattering of applause broke out. But it had by now been a long morning and the elephant could no longer wait. With a deep sigh, it raised its tail and demonstrated what it thought about the proceedings, all over the royal carpet.

Now the four blind men began to argue with one another over who was right and who should win the prize. Strong words were exchanged, fists flew, and things would have become quite unpleasant had at that point the sound of deep laughter not begun to echo around the throne room. The king was roaring with uncontrollable mirth.

'You fools,' he laughed, 'you poor, deluded fools! Do you not see that you are *all* right, for each of you had but one *part* of the elephant. If instead of arguing you had pooled your knowledge, you might have won the prize and shared it. As it is, I shall keep my money, and spend it on a good carpet-cleaning service.'

How to disagree well

The story of the four blind men and the elephant is over 2,500 years old and has been retold hundreds of times. First popularized for Western audiences in a famous poem by John Godfrey Saxe in 1872, the parable has frequently been applied to the question of truth and

---

1 A popular joke among elephants runs like this: 'What are human beings like?' To which the answer is: 'If they're not careful, flat.'

17

exclusivity. Just as each of the blind men mistakenly and arrogantly (and in one case painfully) proclaimed that he alone had correctly discerned the nature of an elephant, so, it is said, whenever human beings proudly proclaim that they uniquely and exclusively have 'The Truth' about a subject, they are probably equally in danger of arrogance and stupidity. Surely it is better to pool our knowledge, to recognize that nobody has the 'whole elephant' and to affirm that everybody has just a part of the truth.

You will therefore not be surprised to learn that the tale of the blind men and the elephant has frequently been applied to religion. Given the tendency of religious people to squabble, fight and even go to war over their doctrinal differences, surely (it is said) the world would be a far more peaceful place if everybody simply stopped making exclusive religious claims and showed a little humility. Why, if only Buddhists and Hindus, Muslims and Christians, Jews and Jedis, and all the other assorted religious believers would simply affirm they had just one part of the truth about God and that other believers had other parts, then the world would be much more harmonious and elephants could enjoy a quiet life.

But is it really the case that the only way to get along is if all parties involved can harmonize, combine or merge their beliefs? Is it not possible to disagree profoundly with somebody and still be friends, or even spouses? I have been married to my wife for more than twenty years and throughout our marriage we have agreed about many things, but we have also had our disagreements. For example, we frequently disagree over whose turn it is to empty the dishwasher, whether it is appropriate to dry wet hiking socks in the toaster or science fiction really is the greatest literary genre ever invented. Based solely on the parable of the blind men and the elephant, we would have to conclude that we cannot have a happy marriage unless we find a way somehow to unify our beliefs. (I did once try suggesting to Astrid that we could just save time by agreeing in advance that I am *always* right, but that suggestion flew about as well as a concrete elephant.)

Yet despite our disagreements, sometimes over minor issues, sometimes over more major ones, we have still had a wonderful marriage which has produced over twenty years of happiness, two beautiful children and only a couple of dents in the plasterwork from flying crockery. In order to build a successful life together, we have not had to pretend we always agree, or attempt to delude ourselves by pretending that we believe essentially the same things, all the while trying to ignore the smell of burning knitwear drifting across the kitchen.

There's no avoiding exclusivity

Thinking carefully about how we handle differences of belief, whether those beliefs are simple domestic ones or whether they are more deeply held convictions, is crucial because however much we try to paper over the differences and steer clear of disagreement, we simply cannot avoid making exclusive truth claims. We cannot avoid saying that what *I* believe is *true*, therefore whoever believes differently is wrong.[2]

Especially when it comes to religious beliefs, even if you try to duck the issue and proclaim, 'All religions are essentially the same' in a well-meaning woolly way, you're *still* making an exclusive truth claim, because the implication surely follows that anybody who says that only *one* religion is true is wrong. You simply cannot avoid the elephant of exclusivity, no matter how carefully you try to spray it with camouflage paint and pretend it isn't there.

But there's a further problem with trying to turn a blind eye to profound differences in belief. Cast your mind back to the story of the blind men and the elephant for a moment and ask yourself who is the most arrogant, the most opinionated person in the story. It's not actually any of the blind men, for all their fighting and arguing.

---

2   If you disagree with me here, then ironically you prove my very point, since you must therefore believe that *I* am wrong and *you* are right.

No, the most arrogant person in the story is actually the king. There he sits, up on his throne, gazing down on the rest of the world from the heights of superiority, idly leafing through *What Pachyderm?* magazine, laughing to himself and thinking: if only those blind fools were as enlightened as me! The whole story hangs precisely on the point that the king can see the whole elephant whereas the blind men are literally – and metaphorically – in the dark.

When somebody tells the parable and applies it to religion, the inherent arrogance of the king transfers to the reteller of the story. Think what the person who uses the story to make a point about religion is *actually* saying: 'If only all the religious people in the world – all those Jews and Sikhs, Buddhists and Muslims, Christians and Hindus – if only they were all as enlightened as me, the world would be a much lovelier place.' The arrogance and superiority are plastered on so thickly here that one could scrape the plaster off and have enough to sculpt a life-size model elephant with. There's an incredible irony in that a story so often told to try to encourage humility about belief is actually rooted in a sense of superiority and arrogance so enormous, it probably has its own gravitational field.

It is arrogance that is the real problem. There is absolutely nothing wrong with believing your beliefs are true; the problem is when you treat those who disagree with you harshly and arrogantly. Cockiness is a problem; confidence and certainty are not.

Desperately seeking certainty

For all the talk about harmonizing and the temptation to water down claims of certainty, I wonder if you've noticed that in most areas of life, confidence and certainty are what most of us want, most of the time. For example, imagine if shortly after boarding a flight to the USA, the captain announced over her public address system, 'I *think* we have enough fuel to make it to New York, but I'm not completely sure. I suggest we take a vote and see if the consensus is that we should take off.' I suspect at this point you would be running for the emergency exit, not nodding happily in agreement and feeling the warm satisfaction that you chose to fly with such a progressive airline. When it comes to aviation, what you want is *certainty*, not warm fuzzy platitudes aimed at affirming everybody's personal beliefs about fuel levels.

Or imagine visiting your doctor complaining of terrible stomach pains, only to be told by him that, far from it being a bad reaction to the goat's cheese soufflé you gobbled late last night, you are actually suffering from a terribly virulent disease that, untreated, would leave you mostly (possibly completely) dead within six months. 'But the good news,' he beams, 'is that there's an incredible new medicine that will cure your condition.'

'Wonderful!' you reply, deeply relieved. 'What drug is it that I need to take?'

'Well . . .' says the doctor hesitantly, toying idly with a small model elephant on his desk, 'here's the thing. As a medical professional I think it's totally inappropriate for me to tell patients what to do. Indeed, it would be highly arrogant for me to claim that my medical training gives me the right to claim I have The Truth when it comes to diagnosis and treatment . . .'

'Huh?' you respond.

'So what about this for an idea?' continues the doctor, warming to his theme. 'How about you come round to my side of the desk and have a rummage in my drawer. I've got lots of different medicines and pills in here – look at them all! Green ones, pink ones, red ones (maybe avoid the blue diamond-shaped ones). What say I give you a box and you can help yourself to whatever pills you feel you'd like? After all, I wouldn't want you to worry that I'm not taking your own beliefs about medicine into consideration . . .'

Now at this point, I suspect most people's reaction would not be to rejoice that they had a wonderfully tolerant, inclusive doctor, but rather to fear they had met a medical madman. What we want in a situation like this are not well-meaning platitudes about inclusivity; what we want is *certainty*.

So, if we want certainty when it comes to aviation, or to medicine, or frankly even to something as simple as crossing the road (either a bus is coming or it isn't), why do people suddenly become all woolly and pliable when it comes to religion and spirituality? After all, surely one of the few insights genuinely common to most of the world's religions is that there is far more to life than just material things – that there is a *spiritual* realm and that how we respond to it is crucial. If that insight is correct, then we are dealing with something potentially way more important than medical diagnoses. Meaning that when it comes to religion, we desperately need certainty as much as (if not more than) we do in any other area of life.

Common objections to religious certainty

Despite that clear need for certainty, one still frequently hears objections to the idea of exclusive truth claims, especially when those claims are made in the area of religion. Although most of these objections have been demolished years ago by professional philosophers, they are still often wheeled – desiccated and covered in cobwebs – out of the cupboard whenever somebody in a conversation happens innocently to reveal deeply held views about God, religion or spirituality and a belief that these views are, in some important way, actually true. So let's tackle some of the most common objections to religious certainty, see why they fail to stand up to scrutiny, and then lock them back in the cupboard and toss away the key.

Fear of fundamentalism

The first objection is the suggestion (often driven by fear of extremism) that claiming your religious beliefs are *really* true (in the same way that it is true that 2+2=4, Paris is the capital of France or

that elephants don't enjoy roller skating) is tantamount to fundamentalism. Usually the word 'fundamentalism' is surrounded by
scare quotes, flashing lights and 'keep out' notices. Of course, nobody
wants to be a *fundamentalist*.[3]

The basic problem here is that most people rarely bother to think
for a moment about what the word 'fundamentalism' actually means
when it is weaponized this way. Usually it is simply a lazy shorthand
for 'This person believes something more confidently than I do', or
it functions as a cheap insult by serving as the opposite of words like
'progressive', 'nice' or 'liberal'. But the fact of the matter is that
everybody is a fundamentalist about something; everybody believes
something to be basically, definitely true. For example, I have secular
friends who are fundamentalist about their belief in human rights,
value and dignity – to which I say, good on them for that. There is
nothing wrong with being a fundamentalist, nothing problematic
about being deeply committed to your beliefs; rather, the questions
should be 'What are those beliefs?' and 'How do they cause you to
behave, especially towards others?'

Growing up, growing pluralist

A second objection to religious certainty is that claiming your
religious beliefs are true is terribly old-fashioned. In the dim and
distant past, people most definitely held to exclusive truths, but then
they spent all their time persecuting or killing one another over
religious dogmas. By contrast, today we live in a tolerant, diverse and
inclusive world, where we no longer spell 'truth' with a capital 'T'
and where the *Oxford English Dictionary*'s international word of the
year for 2016, 'post-truth', is worn by many as a badge of pride.

There are a number of problems here, not least (as we saw above)
that we don't tend to think this way about truth when it comes to
mathematics, navigation, medicine, history or ethics (or in the case

---

3 Unless one is buying tickets for a mind-reading act, in which case, paying to fund a
mentalist is considered to be perfectly fine.

of the last two, sometimes both combined: just try suggesting to somebody that the African slave trade, both the Western trade run by Europeans and the Eastern trade run by Arab Muslims, wasn't actually wrong. Our twenty-first-century penchant for criticizing the immorality of our ancestors really does assume that we can know, historically and morally, what is True). In short, it seems to be only in the realm of religion and spirituality that our thinking turns to raspberry jelly.

Nevertheless, this sloppy thinking has spread widely in our culture, where many people now naturally incline towards soundbites like 'That may be true for you; it's not true for me.' But I wonder if one thing that the ancients knew and that we are in danger of forgetting is that truth is, by its nature, *external* to us. Truth seems to be something we *discover* – like the moon, or the source of the Nile, or the sharp edge of the Lego brick under the heel in the darkened lounge at midnight – rather than something we make up for ourselves as we go along.

But where does that leave the very modern virtue of 'tolerance'? Well, I also wonder whether it is actually highly questionable if that concept really has the load-bearing capacity that is often assumed in our culture. I sometimes like to cause consternation when I speak in places like university campuses by casually remarking that if I could remove one word from the dictionary, I would remove the word 'tolerance'. Why? Because, simply, 'tolerance' is something we extend to things that are beneath us: we tolerate a three-year-old who eats so messily it is tempting to load him into the dishwasher along with the plates; we tolerate the family dog when it chews the sofa for the third time in a week. But adults who are our equals? I would suggest that 'tolerance' is an incredibly patronizing word to reach for at this point; maybe words like 'respect', 'listening' and 'dialogue' are far more appropriate.

That our culture is in danger of forgetting this means that maybe we are not living in such an enlightened age after all. Indeed, for all our tendency to pride ourselves on our diversity and inclusivity, a moment's glance at the rat's nest that is social media on an average day reveals that we live very much in an age where people believe they are right and their enemies are heretics, whether the discussion concerns religion, politics, race, sexuality, gender or cricket.

The ancient world that we are so quick to look down on was arguably much more diverse than the world today. In Greco-Roman society, many people worshipped a plethora of gods and goddesses. If you discovered a new one, you didn't abandon your old beliefs; you simply added the new deity to your existing set of household gods. Yet, just like today, that pluralism and diversity was often cynically encouraged for political ends. It was very convenient for Caesar, for example, to encourage the idea that all the different gods in the world were interchangeable and equivalent, as it made it much easier to deal with the peoples of countries he had conquered.[4]

Constrained by culture

A third objection sometimes made to those who boldly claim to have certainty in matters of religion is to suggest that such people only believe what they believe because of their upbringing. As Lady Gaga might have said to the Swedish Christian: 'You only believe because you were Björn this way.'

Like many soundbites, there is *some* truth to this: if you were born in Saudi Arabia you are more likely to be a Muslim, in North Korea more likely to be an atheist, in Wales less likely to believe in vowels. But at the same time, you can push this idea too far: if you were born in medieval Europe prior to the late seventeenth century, you were likely to believe that the sun moved round the earth; and if you were born in the modern Western world, you are more likely to believe that where you are born affects what you believe. See the

4 See Tom Holland, *Dominion: The making of the Western mind* (London: Little, Brown, 2019), p. 31.

25

problem? For sure, your place and time of birth no doubt affect *what* you believe, but they cannot tell us whether those beliefs are true (or false).

Nor does the culture into which you were born or the family in which you grew up necessarily constrain you from *changing* your beliefs or, in the case of religion, converting to a different faith altogether. I have many friends who are former Muslims, such as my late friend Nabeel Qureshi. Nabeel was born in Pakistan and was brought up in a devoutly Muslim family, yet became a Christian in his twenties after becoming thoroughly convinced that the claims of Jesus and of Christianity were far more persuasive than those of Muhammad and Islam.[5] When you look at conversion patterns today, it is striking that when it comes to Christianity, the fastest-growing churches are not in the Western world – those countries once considered 'Christendom' – but are found in places like the Middle East, Africa and South America.

Observing these patterns, the African theologian Lamin Sanneh once remarked on a fascinating historical tend.[6] When you consider most of the world's oldest and largest religions, they are either still located in or very deeply orientated towards the region of the world in which they began. Islam, for example, is still at its heart an Arab religion: while it has spread widely, through both conquest and conversion, Muslims still pray their set daily prayers in Arabic, facing Mecca, and the Qur'an is only considered sacred scripture when read in Arabic. Fourteen hundred years after the death of Muhammad, Arabia is still, theologically and practically, the centre of the Islamic faith. Similarly, consider Buddhism. Despite its wide geographical spread, during which it has morphed into a variety of different forms, the fact remains that the world

---

5 You can read his story in Nabeel Qureshi, *Seeking Allah, Finding Jesus: A devout Muslim encounters Christianity*, 3rd edn (Grand Rapids, MI: Zondervan, 2018).

6 See Lamin Sanneh, *Whose Religion Is Christianity? The gospel beyond the West* (Grand Rapids, MI: Eerdmans, 2003), especially the introduction and ch. 1.

centre of Buddhism remains South-East Asia – with almost 99% of the half a billion Buddhists on the planet found in that part of the world.[7]

By contrast, throughout its two-thousand-year history, Christianity has continually shifted its cultural centre. It began as a Middle Eastern faith before fanning out along the Roman roads and trade routes. Before long, it had become in part an African faith, with many of the brightest minds in early Christianity coming from North Africa. Then it became a European faith, before becoming, as settlers and explorers took it across the seas, a North American faith. But now the patterns are changing again and, with the huge growth of Christianity in Latin America, Africa, Asia and the Middle East, Christianity's balance is now shifting from the northern hemisphere to the southern.[8] Christianity has never been wedded to one specific culture in the same way as a religion like Islam or Buddhism.

Imagine no religious strife

There is one final objection that is commonly heard to the claim, 'I believe my religious beliefs are definitely, absolutely, uniquely true', and it's what we might term the John Lennon Objection. In one of the most famous songs ever penned by the bearded Liverpudlian songsmith, 'Imagine', Lennon asks us to contemplate a world free of religion, a world that, in consequence, would see everybody living in peace, harmony and oneness.[9] In an interview for *Playboy* magazine, Lennon explained the rationale behind the song:

---

7 See 'Household patterns by religion', Pew Research Center, 12 December 2019, <www.pewforum.org/2019/12/12/household-patterns-by-religion>.

8 See Philip Jenkins, *The Next Christendom: The coming of global Christianity*, 3rd edn (Oxford: Oxford University Press, 2011).

9 The lyrics can be found at <www.metrolyrics.com/imagine-lyrics-john-lennon.html>. Ironically, given that 'Imagine' also calls for an end to greed and possessions, I can't actually quote the lyrics without paying hundreds of pounds per line. It's a shame that Lennon never found the time to write a fourth verse, ideally beginning 'Imagine no double standards . . .'.

Dick Gregory gave Yoko and me a little kind of prayer book. It is in the Christian idiom, but you can apply it anywhere. It is the concept of positive prayer. If you want to get a car, get the car keys. Get it? 'Imagine' is saying that. If you can *imagine* a world at peace, with no denominations of religion – not without religion but without this my-God-is-bigger-than-your-God thing – then it can be true ... The World Church called me once and asked, 'Can we use the lyrics to "Imagine" and just change it to "Imagine *one* religion"?' That showed they didn't understand it at all. It would defeat the whole purpose of the song, the whole idea.[10]

Similar sentiments are expressed by Miroslav Volf, whom we met briefly in chapter 1. In his book *Allah: A Christian response*, Volf pleads passionately for readers to embrace the idea that Muslims and Christians worship the same god, because he believes that adopting such a view will lead to greater peace and harmony. Volf grew up in Yugoslavia, a country historically riven by religious sectarianism and violence (not least between Muslims and Christians), and so his plea for peace has a particular poignancy to it.[11]

While the desire for a world that is more peaceful and harmonious is laudable, there are some fairly major problems with assuming that the way to get there is by downplaying exclusive religious truth claims and harmonizing beliefs. For example, Volf's suggestion that affirming that people worship the same god would lead to peace is somewhat undercut by the 1,400 years of violence between the major Muslim sects, the Sunni and the Shia, all of whose members would claim to believe in the same god, namely Allah. Also, if peace is only possible between people who affirm that each is worshipping the same deity, does that mean peace is unattainable between religious

---

10 David Sheff, *All We Are Saying: The last major interview with John Lennon and Yoko Ono* (New York: St Martin's Press, 1981), pp. 212–213.
11 Miroslav Volf, *Allah: A Christian response* (New York: HarperOne, 2011), pp. 1–5.

people and atheists (who would claim to worship nothing), or between Christians, Jews and Muslims (who are monotheists) and Hindus (who are not)?

Similarly, the old secular idea that a world free of religion would necessarily be a more peaceful one seems, from the perspective of the second decade of the twenty-first century, to be woefully and ludicrously naive. The current collection of countries that have tried to create godless, secular utopias (often imposing their no-religion-permitted ideas by coercion) reads like a masochist's bucket list: North Korea, Myanmar, China and so forth. Similarly, countries that have tried to bring peace by imposing just one religion (such as Saudi Arabia) usually top the list of global human rights offenders.[12]

Neither expunging religion nor forcibly unifying religion seems to be a recipe for success. And even in stable, liberal democracies, pretending that there is agreement in order to somehow promote harmony, friendship or inclusion often fails, because the unity or cohesion that appears at first to be produced is only skin deep. Maybe it is time we stopped being afraid of differences. As Lamin Sanneh remarks:

> [People are] often confused by the view that difference is threatening, fanatical, harmful, and negative while uniform agreement is sound, inclusive, and enlightened. If that were true, we would all be condemned to sameness, uniformity, and conformity. In light of intercommunal conflicts, intrafamily feuds, and the truculence that often arise in the same race, household, or national or faith community, we arrive at a pretty pass when we approach the world in defiance of difference, or in a misguided optimism about agreement . . . People

---

12 See Brian J. Grim and Roger Finke, *The Price of Freedom Denied: Religious persecution and conflict in the twenty-first century* (Cambridge: Cambridge University Press, 2011).

often fight because they want the same thing, or make peace because they embrace difference.[13]

Somehow we need a way to get on despite our differences, to learn not to be threatened by those who hold very different beliefs, but to see those as an opportunity to learn. Perhaps the way to solve some of the tensions in our world is not by eradicating confidence and conviction, but by promoting kindness, especially towards those whose views do not harmonize or align with our own.

Haunted by faith

Despite the fact that these objections to religious certainty fall flat, I can appreciate the motivation that often causes people to raise them: the desire to avoid being unkind to others or excluding them. But if compassion is one emotion underpinning pluralism, there's another, equally powerful emotion, that I see increasingly often in Western culture, and that's *fear of getting it wrong*.

Increasingly I meet people whose story goes a bit like this. They were raised in nominally secular homes and for most of their lives gave little thought to religion, faith or spirituality. But then they began to question some of the assumptions of Western culture, perhaps began to wonder if human beings are more than just atoms and particles, or if life has more to offer than unfettered consumption and casual hedonism, maybe started to ponder whether there is meaning and purpose to be found.

Winifred Gallagher is a journalist who has written for various magazines, including *Rolling Stone*, *Harper's* and *The Atlantic*. A few years ago she published a book, *Working on God*, which described her own rediscovery of spiritual things, a trend that she sees more widely in our culture:

---

13 Sanneh, *Whose Religion*, p. 6.

The only way to describe the new phenomenon I am observing is to coin a new phrase: spiritual agnostics. We have regarded religion as belief in unbelievable things. Our trusted tools of intellect and learning have deconstructed religious belief. But we're finding that we have inexplicable feelings. We wonder: Is this true? Is this all there is? I have tried to muffle this question in all the accustomed ways all my life: love, achievement, stuff, and therapy. I tried to muffle it by writing two books on science. By middle age, I have wearily recognized that religion is the only road I have not taken in pursuit of the answer. We hate religion but we're haunted by faith.[14]

In a similar vein, the Canadian philosopher Charles Taylor, in his book *A Secular Age*, describes how countries like Canada and the UK, despite increasingly turning away from religion, are nevertheless haunted by 'ghosts of transcendence' – the constant reminders that life throws up that maybe the spiritual realm is one we need to attend to.[15] The more you encounter and think about things like beauty, meaning, purpose, identity, value, truth and justice, the more you are drawn to the realization that there is a spiritual as well as a material component to life.

But now the problems start. Once you work out that there *is* a spiritual realm and maybe the time has come to think about it, you look around and discover that there are all these *different* religions. Hundreds of different belief systems with their different scriptures, doctrines, beliefs and practices. They all say very different things and it is fairly obvious that they cannot all be right. So how do you choose? The sheer panoply of options leads some people at this point

---

14 Cited in Peter A. Georgescu, 'Exchange religion for faith', *Huffington Post*, 14 November 2013, <www.huffingtonpost.com/peter-a-georgescu/religion-and-faith_b_4265454.html>.

15 See Charles Taylor, *A Secular Age* (Cambridge, MA: Belknap Press, 2007), especially ch. 9. Taylor is a complex, lengthy and difficult read; a helpful and accessible guide to his thought is James K. A. Smith, *How (Not) to Be Secular: Reading Charles Taylor* (Grand Rapids, MI: Eerdmans, 2014); see especially pp. 3–9.

to panic or paralysis. At which point an inner voice says, 'Maybe all religions are essentially the same', and in a soothing tone pours oil on the troubled waters of your thoughts and allows you to push uncomfortable questions about 'Truth' to the back of your mind.

The problem is that sometimes soothing voices can be lullabies; sometimes they can be siren voices, luring us on to the rocks. And if spiritual realities *really* matter, if it turns out to be the case that knowing the right thing about God is as important as (if not more important than) knowing whether your transatlantic flight is fully fuelled, whether the doctor has prescribed the right medicine, or whether there really is a bus coming before you step on to the crossing, then maybe we need to do the hard work of sifting religious truth from religious fiction.

I want to suggest that the good news is there is a way through the maze of religious options. With a little effort, it is possible to easily compare the claims and teaching of different faiths. You don't need to examine all the religions of the world at once, either: you can begin with the biggest, most likely candidates. Christianity and Islam are the world's two largest religions, with over 4 billion people in the world identifying as followers. Both Christianity and Islam are also rooted in history, making claims that can, in many cases, be tested. But there is also, as we saw in chapter 1, terrible confusion around them, with many people assuming they are more or less identical, especially in what they teach about God. But is that *really* the case? That's what we will be exploring in the rest of this book, and I hope by now that if Christianity and Islam do turn out to be profoundly different, everything you have read in this chapter has reassured you that *difference* is nothing to be afraid of.

So how might we properly compare religious traditions like Christianity and Islam? In the next chapter, we'll discover, with the help of a popular board game, that the task is easier than you might think.

Key takeaways

- There is nothing wrong with having certainty that your religious beliefs are true. After all, in most of life, certainty is what we want ('Will the plank across the river hold my weight?'). What matters is how we treat those with whom we disagree – that we display kindness along with confidence.

- Tolerance is not a virtue. We normally 'tolerate' things or people who are unable to measure up to our standard (we tolerate the naughty toddler or the badly behaved family pet). When dealing with adults, those who are our equals, we instead need to be listening to, respecting and dialoguing with them.

- The popular idea that a religion-free world would be more peaceful is a secular myth. It can be dissolved by looking at history (for example, Stalin's Russia, Pol Pot's Cambodia) or by looking at atheistic countries today such as North Korea, Myanmar or China.

- The family you were born into, and the country and culture in which you grew up, affect but do not determine your religious beliefs. Conversion stories, such as the many accounts of Muslims who have become Christians, show that it is perfectly possible to change your beliefs.

3

Life, the universe and everything

Four questions for comparing and contrasting beliefs

The part of south London where I grew up was very tough. Murderers roamed the streets. Horrific crimes took place on a daily basis (sometimes even several times a day if it was a wet weekend, the local swimming pool was shut and my brother, sister and I were confined to the house).

As kids, my younger siblings and I adored board games and spent many happy hours playing them. Beginning with the preschool joys of Snakes and Ladders, we soon graduated to but quickly exhausted the possibilities of Monopoly (we once made a game last for almost a week by introducing an early version of quantitative easing). We then discovered that we weren't clever or geeky enough for chess and finally landed on Cluedo as our firm favourite.

The premise of the game is simple. It begins with the discovery of a murder victim, the aptly named Mr Boddy,[1] ruthlessly dispatched by an unknown assailant. Players compete to see who can be the first to solve the crime, deducing the identity of the cunning killer, the weapon that finished off the unfortunate victim, and the room in Mr Boddy's rambling mansion where the dastardly deed took place.

Once the game is afoot, players take turns to propose their solutions to the crime, offering up a theory that seeks to answer three basic questions: 'Who did it?', 'Where did they do it?' and 'What weapon was used?' Those three basic questions underpin the entire

---

1   In some editions he's called Dr Black, a futile attempt at changing his name to something that tempted fate less. Perhaps he should have tried calling himself Mr Longevity.

game and easily allow you to compare, contrast and test competing theories about the crime.

For example, if you announce, 'The killer was Miss Scarlet, using the dagger, in the conservatory', and I disagree, stating that I believe it was 'Professor Putin, with the nerve agent, in the potting shed', then we can immediately notice a few things. First, we cannot *both* be correct: our two theories disagree on every key detail and cannot both be right. Second, despite our fundamental differences, we are still both trying to answer the same basic questions; we agree about the *questions* – we just disagree about the *answers*. (And third, with theories like mine, I should probably avoid holidaying in Moscow.)

What in the world is a world view?

Just as there is a basic set of questions underpinning the board game Cluedo – questions that we can put to theories about imaginary crimes – so there are basic questions that we can use in the real world, in particular questions that we can put to world views to help us compare, contrast and assess them.

If you are unfamiliar with the term 'world view', the concept is simple and straightforward. Your world view is your deepest understanding of how the world works, what life is all about and what is really real. It influences what you think about almost everything in life and affects the entire way you see the world: shaping your assumptions, prejudices and preferences; forming your decisions and choices, whether in voting, morality or economics.

Your world view also contributes significantly towards your identity, answering those all-important questions about you and your place in the world. This is true whether your world view is a *religious* one – for example, if you are a Christian or a Muslim – or it is a *secular* one, such as atheism. (Although many atheists are resistant to the idea that their atheism might be considered a religion,[2] it most certainly is a world view, often forming part of their identity.)

However, whether your world view is religious or secular, you rarely think about it or notice it because it is the very nature of a world view to be all-encompassing. In some ways, it's like the story of the two young fish who are merrily swimming along one day when they pass an older fish who remarks, 'Morning, lads. How's the water?' The two younger fish carry on swimming for a while before one finally turns to the other and asks, 'Hey, Stanley, what the heck is water?'[3] Just as fish do not notice the water they are swimming around in, so we rarely pause and pay attention to our world view.

Questioning our foundations

Sometimes it can be incredibly helpful to think about our world view, to examine the foundations, to notice the 'water' in which we live. And just as there were basic questions in Cluedo for assessing theories about the crime, so when it comes to comparing, contrasting and assessing world views there is a simple set of basic questions we can use. We can ask these questions of ourselves and of others, and we can put them to every world view – whether that's Christianity, Islam or even secular atheism.

In Cluedo we had three questions. When it comes to world views, I think there are *four* very helpful questions we can ask.[4]

1 Is there a god (and what is god like)?
2 Who and what are human beings?

---

2 See the extended argument in chapter 2 of Andy Bannister, *The Atheist Who Didn't Exist: Or: the dreadful consequences of bad arguments* (Oxford: Monarch, 2015), showing why atheism should be considered (at least in many cases) a 'religion'.

3 See David Foster Wallace, *This Is Water: Some thoughts, delivered on a significant occasion, about living a compassionate life* (New York: Little, Brown, 2009), pp. 5–6.

4 I have slightly adapted these from the list offered in N. T. Wright, *The New Testament and the People of God*, Christian Origins and the Question of God, vol. 1 (London: SPCK, 2001 [1992]), pp. 132–133.

3 What is wrong with the world?

4 What's the solution?

When talking to somebody I have just met, I usually like to begin with the last two questions on that list, simply because in my experience *everybody*, no matter whether he or she is religious, secular or miscellaneous, has fairly strong opinions about what the problems are in the world – and in many cases equally strong views about what the solutions are. I recall once taking part in a debate on science and religion at the University of Aberdeen in Scotland with a feisty atheist professor. David began his presentation by castigating religions for wanting to see the world as 'broken' or in need of 'salvation', whereas, he retorted, 'I think the world is pretty damn near perfect as it is.' But then within five minutes David was busy listing all the things he thought were wrong with the world (such as poverty, pollution, overpopulation and possibly folk music) and explaining in glowing terms how science, rather than religion, would solve all of these problems eventually.

Everybody, no matter what world view he or she has, thinks *something* is wrong with the world and has some opinion about the solution. But while those questions are a great starting point, they lead naturally and inexorably to the first two questions on the list – simply because it is those questions about God and about humanity that most effectively get to the heart of what somebody thinks is going on with the world. What you think about God and what you think about humanity will powerfully shape what you think is wrong with the world and what you believe the solutions might be.

To show how these four world-view questions work in practice, let's experiment by applying them to atheism. Atheism, especially in its modern varieties, is very much a world view,[5] so how would secular atheism answer our world-view questions? Let's take a look:

---

5 See the discussion in John Gray, *Seven Types of Atheism* (London: Allen Lane, 2018), chs. 1–3. Gray, an atheist himself, goes so far as to remark that much of contemporary atheism and humanism is 'mostly composed of repressed religion' (p. 72).

1 Is there a god and, if so, what is god like? My atheist friends would answer clearly in the negative: there is no god of any kind. (Although it can still be enlightening to ask them the second half of the question: 'What kind of god, specifically, is it that you *don't* believe in?')

2 Who and what are human beings? Since there is no god, matter is the ultimate reality, and so if my atheist friends are being consistent, they will reply by saying something along these lines: 'Humans are simply the undesigned, unintended product of time plus chance plus natural selection.' In other words, we are merely the stuff of which we are made. Indeed as the co-discoverer of DNA, Francis Crick, a committed atheist, starkly put it:

> 'You', your joys and your sorrows, your memories and your ambitions, your sense of personal identity and free will, are in fact no more than the behavior of a vast assembly of nerve cells and their associated molecules. As Lewis Carroll's Alice might have phrased it: 'You're nothing but a pack of neurons.'[6]

But the story doesn't end there. For many atheists, especially those who prefer the label 'humanist', human beings are also bearers of value, dignity and rights.

3 What is wrong with the world? This is a fascinating question to put to atheist friends as the answers are often more varied. Religion is commonly mentioned (think John Lennon and his famous song), as are politicians (usually the issue is that the wrong kind are in power; if only *my* kind had been voted in). Environmental issues are increasingly mentioned here too, along with a rogues' gallery of bankers, lawyers and greedy capitalists, who we all know are a

---

6 Francis Crick, *The Astonishing Hypothesis: The scientific search for the soul* (New York: Touchstone, 1994), p. 1.

terrible lot. All the world's problems can be laid at the feet of these kind of people – but of course there's nothing *spiritually* wrong with us, because there is no spiritual realm (see question 1).

4 What's the solution? My atheist friends tend to offer answers that boil down to the idea that humans are clever enough and ingenious enough to work it out eventually. Throw enough politics (of the right kind), or science, or technology, or health care, or education, or justice, or caffeine at the problems and we can eventually navigate our way to utopia, or at least somewhere roughly in the same ball-park. There may not be a heaven, but we can build something approximating it here on earth given enough resources – or if that fails, eventually digitize ourselves and upload our personalities to the internet and live for ever.

Here is not the place to explore whether or not these atheist answers to the four world-view questions are true or coherent (we might ask, for example, whether the claim that human beings are just matter sits very easily with the belief that they have rights, value and dignity).[7] For now, the point is simply to show how asking these four questions helps us map out in more detail what is going on when somebody says, 'I am an atheist.' When you meet somebody who describes himself or herself this way, don't let the matter rest there: press into the four world-view questions and explore more deeply the foundations of what he or she believes. If you use that label for yourself, go through the same process.

The advantage of doing this is twofold. First, it encourages real thought about what individuals mean when they call themselves 'atheist'. But, second, mapping a belief like this makes it far easier to

---

7   There have been many excellent books written subjecting atheism to rigorous critique. For example, see Holly Ordway, *Not God's Type: An atheist academic lays down her arms* (San Francisco, CA: Ignatius Press, 2014); John Lennox, *Gunning for God: Why the new atheists are missing the target* (Oxford: Lion, 2011).

compare and contrast it with other world views that compete with atheism in the marketplace of ideas.

Comparing Christianity and Islam

For all the attention that atheism gets in the West, globally atheism is in slow, possibly terminal, decline. Rather, it is religious world views like Christianity and Islam, which between them account for almost two thirds of the world's population, that will shape the lives of individuals and societies in the twenty-first century.

Now, as we saw in chapter 1, it is very tempting when we think of Christianity and Islam to focus on the superficial similarities, perhaps lumping them together under the generic catch-all term 'religion' (a word whose definition is still heavily contested among academics, who like any excuse for a good argument). Or we indulge in glib generalities, opining that Muslims and Christians are both 'monotheistic', both believe in some kind of 'afterlife', and neither are likely to have 'I ♥ Richard Dawkins' stickers on their car bumper.

But what if those vague similarities mask major differences? What if, rather than being superficially different but fundamentally the same, Islam and Christianity are actually *fundamentally* different with just *superficial* similarities? Unless one is resigned to being terminally lazy or perpetually dim-witted, this may be a fairly important thing to know. Which is precisely where our four world-view questions come riding over the horizon to our aid.

By applying these four questions to Christianity and Islam, we have a real possibility of getting to the heart of the stories about reality that both Christians and Muslims are trying to tell. The questions are also basic enough that they neatly bypass the issue of different sects and denominations (for example, Sunni versus Shiite, or Baptist versus Presbyterian) by digging down to the fundamental foundations that glue together Christians and bind together Muslims, despite the wonderful and rich variety of the adherents of these two religions.

1 Is there a god and, if so, what is god like? Muslims and Christians would agree that there is a god, but the second half of the question is crucial: what, precisely, is god like? Do Muslims and Christians also agree on the nature and character of that god? In short, do they worship the *same* god, or is Allah (the name the Qur'an uses for god) very different from Yahweh (the name by which the god of the Bible identifies himself)?

2 Who and what are human beings? Muslims and Christians would agree that human beings are created; we are not merely the result of natural forces, croutons that have bubbled up from the primordial soup. But can we go deeper and say more? What do Muslims and Christians think it means to be a human? What is our relationship to god, for example?

3 What is wrong with the world? Most people think that all religions operate with a similar core narrative: god wants us to be nice and do what he says, whereas humans often do precisely the opposite (especially the really naughty people, those who like causing pain, like psychopaths and dentists). But is this *actually* what Islam and Christianity say? Do Muslims and Christians agree in their diagnosis of what's gone wrong? And what do their diagnoses of the problem tell us about god?

4 What's the solution? Again, most people think that all religions say that because the problem is disobedience, the solution is obedience. In this simplistic caricature, God says something like: 'Hey, folks, here are some laws. Listen up, knuckle down and work hard at them – and if you rack up enough moral points, you get to go to heaven! If not, it's the other place (by which I don't mean Belgium).'

But is this *really* what Islam and Christianity are saying? Do they agree that the solution is obedience, the goal is moral point-scoring, and the destination we're aiming at is an eternal party in heaven?

So that, ladies and gentlemen, is our roadmap for the next four chapters. One at a time, we will take each of the world-view questions and unpack what Islam and Christianity have to say about them. We'll uncover some similarities, but we'll also discover some deep differences and, as we explore the foundations of Christianity and Islam, we will continue to ask ourselves about the *relationship* between these two great religious traditions. Are they two takes on the same story – two slightly different flavours of ice-cream, but essentially the same frozen dairy snack – or are we comparing not so much apples and oranges here as two entirely different food groups?[8]

The author Os Guinness once remarked that 'contrast is the mother of clarity', by which he meant that when you carefully compare and contrast two things, you often understand both of them better. I think this is especially the case when we are pushing back against a default assumption that the two things are basically the same. As we compare Christianity's and Islam's answers to these four foundational world-view questions, I hope that the journey will bring into sharp focus the very unique perspectives these two religions have on life's deepest questions. So let's begin with the most important, the most basic, the most crucial and foundational question of all: 'Is there a god and, if so, what is god like?'

Key takeaways

- Everybody has a world view, no matter if a person is religious or secular. A world view is the basic way that you see the world

---

8 For the record, ice-cream is definitely a food group.

and it shapes everything: your assumptions, prejudices, politics and preferences.

- We can easily compare and contrast world views by asking four basic questions.
    - Is there a god (and what is god like)?
    - Who and what are human beings?
    - What's wrong with the world?
    - What's the solution?

4

Will the real God please stand up?

Comparing the Bible's and the Qur'an's views of God

Despite their innocent appearance, words can sometimes be slippery things. For example, it is tempting to assume unquestioningly that when someone uses a word we are familiar with, he or she means precisely the same thing by it as we do. Hilarity, confusion and sometimes even minor wars have resulted from the discovery that the other person, when using a certain word, actually meant something entirely different from what you thought.

I first really noticed this phenomenon during my years living in Canada. Soon after moving to Toronto from Oxford, I quickly discovered that my Canadian friends meant quite different things by words like 'pants' (equivalent to the British word 'underpants', a not unimportant distinction if you wish to avoid embarrassment or arrest), 'football' (the British English equivalent of what the Canadians call 'football' is probably 'melee') and 'large' (a term that if foolishly used when ordering lunch in some Canadian fast-food outlets can result in enough calories to feed a family of four).

When a word is not defined properly, things can quickly get confusing. When my son Christopher was tiny, he loved tractors and 'tractor' was one of the first words he learned to say clearly. However, the problem (especially for visiting friends unaware of Christopher's linguistic flexibility) was that he would happily use the word 'tractor' to denote anything with wheels: everything from farm vehicles to cars, to lorries, to – on one memorable occasion – a mobility scooter.

Whatever words we are using, it is important to clarify exactly what we mean by them. This is especially true if the word in question is a powerful and fundamentally important one: a word like 'god', for example. When we ask, 'Do Muslims and Christians worship the same god?', we must not lazily assume that everybody in the conversation means exactly the same thing by the word 'god'; otherwise, the misunderstandings pile up like a heap of lemmings at the foot of a cliff. So let's back up a little and ask what Muslims and Christians actually *mean* by the word 'god'.

We can begin by observing that Muslims and Christians are not using the word 'god' in some kind of vague, theoretical way. For devout believers, the 'god' is not a mere idea, nor some neutral and random fact about the universe. Christians and Muslims don't wander around thinking things like: hey ho, Callisto is the second-largest moon of Jupiter; Einstein invented the cat flap; oh, and God exists. God is not just an additional fact *about* reality; rather, God is the foundation underpinning the whole *of* reality.

The Bible pulls no punches here, pointing out that there is nothing commendable about merely *believing* that God exists: 'You believe that there is one God. Good! Even the demons believe that – and shudder' (James 2:19).

Neither the Bible nor the Qur'an is particularly interested in the purely theoretical question of *whether* God exists; rather, they consider the infinitely more important question to be: what is God like? What is God's character, nature and identity? What are his attributes? In short, rather than '*Is* there a god?', we should instead be asking the question '*Who* is god?'

Mistaken identities

For those who think that Muslims and Christians are talking about the same god, any differences in who they believe God is are explained as being simply different perceptions of the same being (rather like the blind men all encountering the same elephant but having different views of it). Or to consider another example: my wife and I have very different views about Leonardo DiCaprio's acting ability. My wife thinks DiCaprio is one of the greatest actors in the world and it's a total travesty that he's not won an Oscar yet; conversely, I think he's totally useless and about as wooden as that plank he failed to clamber on to at the end of *Titanic*. If you were to hear us both talking about DiCaprio, it might sound as if we were talking about two completely different people; but although our opinions of him are wildly different, we are still talking about someone with the same *identity*. Is something similar going on with Muslims, Christians and God – or are the differences between the Bible's and the Qur'an's view of God much more fundamental? Could it be that Christians and Muslims agree about God's existence but *disagree* about his identity?

Once you untangle the mere fact of God's existence from the question of what God is like – once you begin thinking about God's character and identity – you quickly stumble across the fact that it is perfectly possible to agree about somebody's *existence* but disagree profoundly about their *identity*. Think back to the example of the Cluedo board game from chapter 3. That entire game is structured around the question of identity: all the players agree that a murderer exists (*somebody* cruelly dispatched the poor, hapless Mr Boddy after he had invited a bunch of psychopaths around for supper while leaving a myriad potential murder weapons liberally scattered around the premises), but until the game is resolved, there will be plenty of disagreement about the identity of the murderer. Once again, we see that there's a difference between existence (clearly a killer exists) and identity (who that killer actually is).

Here's another thought experiment. Imagine that you and I bump into each other at a coffee shop and get chatting. During the conversation, I mention where I grew up and went to school and, amazingly, it turns out that you went to the same school as I did. In passing I mention my friend Ahmad, to which you respond, 'No way! I was friends with him too! We met playing rugby.'

I explain this cannot possibly be correct, as *my* friend Ahmad hated rugby: he was geekier and much more partial to chess.

'Geeky?' you say, puzzled, explaining how your friend Ahmad hated academic subjects and preferred sport, especially basketball, as his being 6 foot 2 really helped.

'Six foot two!' I exclaim. 'My friend Ahmad was the shortest guy at school!'

As we continue to discover further differences, it becomes increasingly apparent that our initial impression was mistaken: yes, there are *some* similarities (the same school, the same number of limbs, even the same first name), but the differences are significant enough to make it clear quite soon that we were not friends with the same person.

Finally, we might think about an example from the world of politics. Suppose that I am having a debate with my friend Kevin about who is the current president of the United States of America. Being sufficiently educated to use the internet, Kevin informs me that the current president is Joe Biden. But I have little time for politics and so I'm slightly out of touch: 'I thought the president was Donald Duck,' I reply. Much as Kevin and I might have a thoroughly entertaining debate about the Disneyfication of politics and about who might make the better president, notice something interesting: we both agree there is a president, yet we disagree over *who* that president is. If you asked, 'Do Andy and Kevin believe in the same president?', clearly the answer is 'No'.[1]

---

1 Boston University professor Stephen Prothero offers another example from politics. Imagine you asked a Communist and a Social Democrat if they both believed in 'politics' and, on hearing the answer 'Yes', you assumed that Communism and Social Democracy were essentially the same. Arguably you have missed something fairly crucial, simply because you forgot to ask the vital question: 'What do you *mean* by the word "politics"?' See Stephen Prothero, *God Is Not One: The eight rival religions that run the world* (New York: HarperOne, 2010), pp. 1 and 9.

In a similar way, it is perfectly possible for Muslims and Christians to agree entirely that God *exists* – even to agree on some of God's functions (creating, ruling, judging). But that's not enough; rather, we must ask about the *identity* of the god that Muslims and Christians believe in and see how well the descriptions line up. If there are only minor differences between Yahweh and Allah, then maybe we have something more akin to the confusion over whether a film star deserves an Oscar. If, however, the differences turn out to be far greater, then we must consider the possibility that Muslims and Christians are potentially talking about two quite different gods.

So let's take a look at five characteristics that are central to the identity of the God of the Bible – crucial aspects of God's character portrayed on page after page of the biblical text – across both the Old and New Testaments. In each case, we will then consider what the Qur'an has to say about these same characteristics and see whether its portrayal of Allah looks at all similar to how the Bible describes Yahweh.

The God of the Bible is relational

The first major characteristic of Yahweh, the God of the Bible, is that he is *relational.* In Genesis, the very first book of the Bible, we read about God calling into existence the whole of creation – everything from planets and stars to oceans and continents, from trees and plants to animals, birds and human beings. So, after all this creative activity, what does God do? Yahweh then steps into creation in order to relate, in person, to the first humans: 'Then they heard the sound of Yahweh God walking in the garden at the windy time of day' (Genesis 3:8 LEB).

Throughout the Old Testament we read of numerous 'theophanies', dramatic moments when God again steps down into creation and relates to human beings personally. One of the most astonishing examples comes in Genesis 15, where God appears to Abram (the original name of the patriarch Abraham) and forms a 'covenant' with him – a deep, serious commitment that goes way beyond a mere promise. In the Ancient Near East of Abram's day, covenants were often marked by a ceremony in which the two parties would cut animal carcases in two and walk between the halves – the symbolism implying, 'If I break my word, may I be torn apart like these animals.' In a sign of Yahweh's incredible willingness to relate to human beings, God is even willing to take part in a covenant-cutting ceremony, passing symbolically between the carcases that Abram has severed: 'And after the sun had gone down and it was dusk, behold, a smoking firepot and a flaming torch passed between those half pieces. On that day Yahweh made a covenant with Abram' (Genesis 15:17–18 LEB).

Time and time again, the Bible emphasizes that as well as being powerful and exalted, Yahweh is also a God who dwells with the lowest of the low. A heavenly king who reigns in power, but also one who is able to stoop down and be present with us:

> For this is what the high and exalted One says –
>   he who lives for ever, whose name is holy:
> 'I live in a high and holy place,
>   but also with the one who is contrite and lowly in spirit . . .'
> (Isaiah 57:15)

The theme of God relating to human beings runs throughout the whole of the Old Testament and onwards into the New Testament, where it reaches its zenith in the person of Jesus Christ who, according to the Bible, was no mere prophet but 'God with us'.[2] As the New Testament repeatedly teaches, if you want to see what God is like, look at Jesus:

---

2 Matthew 1:23.

[Jesus Christ] is the image of the invisible God, the firstborn over all creation . . . For God was pleased to have all his fullness dwell in him, and through him to reconcile to himself all things, whether things on earth or things in heaven, by making peace through his blood, shed on the cross.
(Colossians 1:15, 19–20)

The biblical theme of God's relationality appears at the *beginning* of history, at creation; it appears in the *middle* of biblical history, in the person of Jesus; and it also appears at the *end* of history, in the Bible's highly relational language of what our eternal future will be like. The future hope offered by the Bible is not a cloud-based party in heaven with angels wielding harps, but rather that we will be raised to eternal life in God's new creation, enjoying an eternity of close relationship with him:

I saw a new heaven and a new earth . . . And I heard a loud voice from the throne saying,

'Behold, the dwelling of God is with humanity,
and he will take up residence with them,
and they will be his people
and God himself will be with them.
And he will wipe away every tear from their eyes,
    and death will not exist any longer,
    and mourning or wailing or pain will not exist
        any longer.
The former things have passed away.'
(Revelation 21:1, 3–4 LEB)

That Yahweh is relational is also shown by the sheer number of relational titles that the Bible uses for God. Yes, God is certainly Lord and King, but he is also described as a father, as a friend, even as a husband. According to Jesus, we can address God simply and intimately as 'Our Father in heaven'.[3]

So what about Allah, the God described by the Qur'an? By far the main emphasis of the Qur'an in its portrayal of God is not his relationality but his distance. Allah is never close and personal, but only ever high and mighty, powerful and transcendent, lofty and distant:

> There is no god but [Allah], the Living, the Everlasting. Slumber seizes Him not, neither sleep; to Him belongs all that is in the heavens and the earth . . . His Throne comprises the heavens and earth; the preserving of them oppresses Him not; He is the All-high, the All-glorious.
> (Q. 2:255)

This theme of Allah's power, transcendence and distance is repeatedly emphasized by the Qur'an.[4] For example, scholars who have carefully studied the Qur'an's Arabic have noticed that the Qur'an is constructed using highly formulaic language, repeated phrases that are returned to time and time again.[5] The frequency of these formulaic phrases gives an insight into the Qur'an's *central* ideas and thus it is noteworthy that the third most common formula in the Qur'an, repeated some fifty times, is the phrase 'Allah is over all things'.

Internationally renowned Muslim scholar Farid Esack sums up this aspect of the Qur'an succinctly: 'Belief in the existence of one

---

3 Matthew 6:9.

4 People will sometimes quote Q. 50:16, which speaks of Allah being 'closer' to a person than his or her 'jugular vein', as an example of Allah's closeness in the Qur'an. But when one reads the entire passage, it is clear that this verse is talking about *judgment*, not relationality: human beings should mind their behaviour, because Allah is literally watching over their shoulder.

5 For an overview of the Qur'an's use of formulaic language, see Andrew Bannister, 'Retelling the tale: a computerised oral-formulaic analysis of the Qur'an' (available on the Academia website at <www.academia.edu/9490706>).

transcendent Creator and the struggle to live with all the implications of that belief may be said to be at the core of the Qur'an's message.'[6]

This emphasis of the Qur'an on Allah's transcendence rather than his closeness to human beings is seen in other ways. For example, the Qur'an frequently retells stories from the Bible and from Jewish and Christian tradition (about a quarter of the Qur'an is made up of this kind of material). As it draws on biblical stories, the Qur'an frequently reshapes them to suit its own theology; as it does this, one theme often edited out or downplayed is God's relationality. Consider the Qur'an's retelling of the story of Adam and Eve in the garden:

> 'O Adam! dwell thou and thy wife in the Garden, and enjoy (its good things) as ye wish: but approach not this tree, or ye run into harm and transgression.'
>
> Then began Satan to whisper suggestions to them, bringing openly before their minds all their shame that was hidden from them (before): he said: 'Your Lord only forbade you this tree, lest ye should become angels or such beings as live for ever.'
>
> And he swore to them both, that he was their sincere adviser.
>
> So by deceit he brought about their fall: when they tasted of the tree, their shame became manifest to them, and they began to sew together the leaves of the garden over their bodies. And their Lord called unto them: 'Did I not forbid you that tree, and tell you that Satan was an avowed enemy unto you?'
> (Q. 7:19–22)

In this qur'anic retelling of the biblical story from Genesis 3, it is fascinating to see which elements have been retained by the Qur'an and which have been dropped or edited. Notably changed is that

---

6 Farid Esack, *The Qur'an: A user's guide* (Oxford: Oneworld, 2005), p. 147, my emphasis.

Allah has been abstracted from the scene; yes, he speaks to the first human couple, but he is no longer portrayed as walking with them in his creation.

Something similar happens with the story of the covenant cutting in Genesis 15. The Qur'an has no real concept of covenant (probably because the idea of God *binding* himself to human beings is considered by the Qur'an to be beneath Allah) and so the story of God, Abraham and the sacrificial animals and birds is turned into a strange little parable about resurrection:

> (Remember) when Abraham said, 'My Lord, show me how You give the dead life.' He said, 'Have you not believed?' He said, 'Yes indeed! But (show me) to satisfy my heart.' He said, 'Take four birds, and take them close to you, then place a piece of them on each hill, (and) then call them. They will come rushing to you. Know that God is mighty, wise.'
> (Q. 2:260)

When it comes to Jesus, the Qur'an demotes him to the status of just another prophet, not the Son of God, and certainly not God-come-in-the-flesh to relate to us. About ninety verses in the Qur'an discuss Jesus, and the Qur'an uses many of them to play down Jesus' role. For example, the Qur'an reports this conversation between Allah and Jesus:

> (Remember) when God said, 'Jesus, son of Mary! Did you say to the people, "Take me and my mother as two gods instead of God (alone)"?' He said, 'Glory to You! It is not for me to say what I have no right (to say). If I had said it, You would have known it. You know what is within me, but I do not know what is within You. Surely You – You are the Knower of the unseen.'
> (Q. 5:116)

Finally, what about 'heaven'? This is an idea that in the Bible is far richer than one word can convey and is deeply relational – Yahweh promising to dwell with his people as he did with Adam and Eve in Eden.[7] The Qur'an certainly speaks much about heaven, painting a vivid picture of a place filled with fruit trees (Q. 2:25), rivers of wine (Q. 47:15), and young women to be enjoyed by male believers (Q. 52:20). Yet nowhere in these descriptions of heaven does the Qur'an promise its readers any kind of relationship with Allah.

In short, for the Qur'an Allah is distant at the *beginning* of history (not walking with Adam and Eve, or covenanting with Abraham); he is absent in the *middle* of history (not coming in the person of Jesus); and he is *missing* from the end of history (heaven has pleasures, but it lacks God's presence).

This emphasis on Allah's distance and transcendence explains why the Qur'an never invites readers into any kind of 'relationship' with God – and it certainly does not permit Muslims to dare to call Allah 'Father'. Indeed, in sura 112,[8] once described by Muhammad as so significant that reciting it is equivalent to reciting a third of the Qur'an,[9] the Qur'an outrightly declares that Allah is not a father and that Allah has no son: '[Allah] has not begotten, and has not been begotten' (Q. 112:3).

Summarizing these crucial differences from the Bible, Muslim philosopher Shabbir Akhtar explains: 'Muslims do not see God as their father ... Men are servants of a just master; they cannot, in orthodox Islam, typically attain any greater degree of intimacy with their creator.'[10]

---

7 See the longer discussion in chapter 7 about the differences between the biblical and qur'anic views of what eternal life will look like.

8 A sura is a chapter or section of the Qur'an.

9 See the hadith recorded in Sahih al-Bukhari 5015.

10 Shabbir Akhtar, *A Faith for All Seasons: Islam and the challenge of the modern world* (Chicago, IL: Ivan R. Dee, 1990), p. 180.

The God of the Bible can be known

We have seen that a major difference between the identity of Yahweh in the Bible and of Allah in the Qur'an is relationality. Now it is only possible to have a relationship with somebody if that person is willing to make himself or herself *known*. Imagine that you are grocery shopping at the local supermarket when suddenly, across the freezer cabinets, you catch a glimpse of the most beautiful (or most handsome) person you have ever seen. The way the light catches her eyes, the flow of her hair, the way she handles that packet of frozen broccoli – all of it is enchanting. You fall instantly in love and begin to make some enquiries: who is this person? Where does she live? How might I start a relationship with her? But the news quickly turns sour: apparently the object of your dreams is the shyest, most socially withdrawn person in the whole of your town. She works from home, never replies to messages, and only occasionally ventures out to shop for food or to attend meetings of the local branch of Agoraphobics Anonymous.[11] In short, any kind of relationship would be impossible.

A relationship is only possible if individuals make themselves known. This is true of human beings and it is also true of God. If God hid himself away in heaven, never revealing himself, then we might know *about* him (we might perhaps know his laws and commands) but we could never know *him*.

The Bible understands this well and so, from beginning to end, describes a God who reveals not just his commandments but also his character and his identity. For example, consider the famous story of Moses and the burning bush in Exodus 3. Moses has fled to the wilderness after murdering an Egyptian slaver and is living as a fugitive. But God has bigger plans for Moses and in a dramatic theophany appears to him in flames of fire and explains how he

---

11 But those are closed-door meetings.

intends to use Moses to rescue the Israelites from slavery. But Moses, a nervous fellow, objects:

> Moses said to God, 'Suppose I go to the Israelites and say to them, "The God of your fathers has sent me to you," and they ask me, "What is his name?" Then what shall I tell them?'
> God said to Moses, 'I AM WHO I AM. This is what you are to say to the Israelites: "I AM has sent me to you."'
> (Exodus 3:13–14)

It is possible to be so overly familiar with this story that we miss how startling it is. For the Hebrew translated here as 'I AM' is 'Yahweh', the personal name for God used in the Bible over 6,500 times. Amazingly, God, the creator and ruler of all things, is willing to make himself known to humans by his very own personal name.

We live in an age where it is common to think of knowledge purely in terms of information; but for the Bible, knowledge is far more about relationship and commitment. And because it is relationship that the God of the Bible desires, Yahweh is willing to make himself known. He says: 'I will give to them a heart to *know* me, that I am Yahweh, and they will be my people, and I will be their God, for they will return to me with the whole of their heart' (Jeremiah 24:7 LEB).[12]

Just as with relationality, so the biblical theme of Yahweh being a God who makes himself known likewise reaches its culmination in Jesus:

> Jesus [said], 'I am the way and the truth and the life. No-one comes to the Father except through me. If you really *knew* me, you would *know* my Father as well. From now on, you do know him and have seen him.'

---

12 All emphasis in quotations from the Bible is mine.

Philip said, 'Lord, show us the Father and that will be enough for us.'

Jesus answered: 'Don't you know me, Philip, even after I have been among you for such a long time? *Anyone who has seen me has seen the Father.*'

(John 14:6–9 NIV 1984)

How does all of this compare with the Qur'an and its portrayal of Allah? The Qur'an certainly talks at length about knowledge. The Arabic words for 'knowing' and 'knowledge' (*'alim* and *'ilm*) occur over 650 times and the Qur'an frequently extols the value of knowledge: 'Say: "Are those who know and those who do not know equal?" Only those with understanding take heed' (Q. 39:9).

Great emphasis is put on right knowledge about God, the Qur'an assuming that the truth about Allah is self-evident: '(There is) no compulsion in religion. The right (course) has become clearly distinguished from error. Whoever disbelieves in [falsehood, idols], and believes in God, has grasped the firmest handle, (which) does not break. God is hearing, knowing' (Q. 2:256).

However, it is striking that in all the hundreds of references to knowledge in the Qur'an, there is no invitation to *know* Allah; rather, what is expected of Muslims is correct belief *about* Allah. As if to underscore this very point, the Qur'an takes the famous biblical story of Moses and the burning bush and removes from it the tender scene where God reveals his own, personal name:

When Moses saw a fire, he said to his family, 'Stay (here). Surely I perceive a fire. Perhaps I shall bring you a flaming torch from it, or I shall find at the fire guidance.' But when he came to it, he was called: 'Moses! Surely I am your Lord, so take off your shoes. Surely you are in the holy wādī of Ṭuwā. I have chosen you, so listen to what is inspired. Surely I am God – (there is) no god but Me. So serve Me, and observe the prayer for My remembrance! Surely the Hour is coming – I almost hide it, so that every person may be repaid for what he strives after. So do not let anyone who does not believe in it, and who (only) follows his (own) desire, keep you from it, or you will be brought to ruin.'

(Q. 20:10–16)

While a few elements of the biblical account are preserved, the heart of the story (God revealing his name to Moses) is gone. Instead, Moses is reminded of good Islamic doctrine, warned of the day of judgment ('The Hour') and told to be wary of disbelievers.

Similarly, the Qur'an takes the person of Jesus (the ultimate example of God's making himself known in the Bible) and downgrades him to being just another messenger:

The Messiah, Jesus, son of Mary, was only a messenger of God, and His word, which He cast into Mary, and a spirit from Him. So believe in God and His messengers, but do not say, 'Three.' Stop! (It will be) better for you. God is only one God. Glory to Him! (Far be it) that He should have a son!

(Q. 4:171)

For the Qur'an, one can know *about* Allah and know that Allah has sent prophets and messengers (such as Jesus) so that human beings might be without excuse. But when it comes to Allah revealing *himself,* that is a line that the Qur'an steadfastly refuses to cross. As the Palestinian Muslim scholar Ismail al-Faruqi put it: 'Allah does not reveal Himself to anyone in any way. Allah reveals only his will . . . Allah does not reveal himself to anyone . . . that is the great difference between Christianity and Islam.'[13]

---

13 Ismail al-Faruqi, *Christian Mission and Islamic Da'wah: Proceedings of the Chambésy Dialogue Consultation* (Leicester: Islamic Foundation, 1982), pp. 47–48.

The God of the Bible is holy

A third characteristic of the Bible's portrayal of God is that Yahweh is *holy*, a word the Bible uses over eighty times to describe God. For example, in the prophet Isaiah's dramatic vision of God in his heavenly temple, Isaiah sees angels calling out:

Holy, holy, holy is Yahweh of hosts!
    The whole earth is full of his glory.
(Isaiah 6:3 LEB)[14]

Over forty times the Old Testament calls Yahweh 'the Holy One of Israel', whose holiness means he is so pure that he cannot tolerate sin in his presence:

Are you not from of old,
    O Yahweh my God, my Holy One? . . .
Your eyes are too pure to see evil,
    and you are not able to look at wrongdoing.
(Habakkuk 1:12–13 LEB)

This connects to a key biblical idea about God's holiness, namely separation. Because Yahweh is holy and because humans are rebellious and sinful, humans are separated from God; this is why Adam and Eve were barred from Eden and why a curtain separated worshippers from the innermost part of the Jewish temple, the holy of holies.[15] Yet God's desire throughout the Bible is not simply for human obedience but that humans might reflect his character and holiness: 'You must be holy, because I, Yahweh your God, am holy' (Leviticus 19:2 LEB).

---

14 Compare Revelation 4:8.
15 2 Chronicles 3:14; Hebrews 9:3.

Jesus echoes this language in his Sermon on the Mount: 'Be perfect, therefore, as your heavenly Father is perfect' (Matthew 5:48). As the New Testament unpacks this theme, it connects it to Jesus' death and resurrection, explaining that because humans cannot live up to this high calling, Jesus has done it for us: 'All have sinned and fall short of the glory of God, and all are justified freely by his grace through the redemption that came by Christ Jesus' (Romans 3:23–24).

So what, then, of the Qur'an? Many people assume that holiness must be a key theme in the Qur'an, a book that many Muslims describe as 'Holy'. Yet the Arabic words for 'holiness'[16] occur only ten times in the Qur'an and four of those are references to 'the Holy Spirit' (traditionally understood by Muslims to be the angel Gabriel). Only three times – literally, just *three* times – does the Qur'an call Allah 'holy'. Here is one example: 'He is God, the One who – (there is no) god but Him – is the King, the Holy One, the Peace, the Faithful, the Preserver, the Mighty, the Sole Ruler, the Magnificent' (Q. 59:23).[17]

Elsewhere, the Qur'an is clear that Allah is the supreme judge who commands obedience and will hold human beings to account for their actions, but the Qur'an does not connect this to the idea of Allah's holiness; it is not because he is too holy to look on sin that Allah judges, but because he is all-powerful: 'Surely your Lord will decide between them by His judgment. He is the Mighty, the Knowing' (Q. 27:78).

Nor is there any equivalent in the Qur'an to the Bible's call to humans to 'be holy as God is holy'; rather, for the Qur'an what matters is human obedience. And when Allah does judge, he does so not out of his character as holy and pure, nor out of any kind of faithfulness to promises or covenants he has made with humanity,

---

16 Based on the Arabic root *qds*.
17 The other references to Allah being holy are Q. 2:30 and Q. 62:1.

but purely arbitrarily, out of his will. As one of the world's foremost qur'anic scholars, Gabriel Said Reynolds, describes it:

> The eternal fate of humans is wholly dependent on Allah's will and cannot be known . . . The point is not that Allah is necessarily kind and gentle, or that he is wrathful and vindictive, but that Allah has the right to do as he pleases.[18]

The God of the Bible is love

The fourth characteristic of Yahweh is that he is a God of *love*. This is an attribute of God identified by the Bible hundreds of times. For example, in what scholars believe to one of the very oldest books of the Bible, Jonah, famous for its namesake's fishy adventure, Jonah throws a tantrum and wails that God has decided not to destroy the wicked city of Nineveh. Jonah had thought God might behave like this because, he says, 'I knew that you are a gracious and compassionate God, slow to anger and *abounding in love*, a God who relents from sending calamity' (Jonah 4:2).

In the Psalms, the hymn book of the Jewish people and the early Christians, the theme of God's love is ever-present, such as in Psalm 136, where twenty-six times we hear the chorus 'His love endures for ever'. Love is one of the ways in which Yahweh self-identifies, such as in the book of Jeremiah where we read of Yahweh saying:

> I have loved you with an everlasting love;
>   I have drawn you with loving-kindness.
> (Jeremiah 31:3 NIV 1984)

When we reach the New Testament, the love of God is a theme to which Jesus repeatedly returned. In one of the most famous verses

---

18 Gabriel Said Reynolds, *Allah: God in the Qur'an* (New Haven, CT: Yale University Press, 2020), p. 140.

in the Gospels, a verse often memorized by Christians because of how beautifully it summarizes the Christian faith, Jesus described the incredible love that God has for all that he has made: 'For God so loved the world that he gave his one and only Son, that whoever believes in him shall not perish but have eternal life' (John 3:16).

But the Bible is not content simply to describe Yahweh as loving. It goes radically further, teaching that God's very essence, his very identity, is love: 'God is love' (1 John 4:16). There is a lot packed into those three little words. The Bible teaches that it is not so much that Yahweh *acts* lovingly, but that he *is* loving. Love is not something God *does*; love is something God *is*. This gives Christians tremendous confidence in their ability to trust God, knowing that the heart of his identity is love. It also reveals why the Bible's teaching that there is one God who exists in three persons – Father, Son and Spirit (what Christians came to call the Trinity) – is so important. For if God was not triune but single and solitary, it would not be possible for him to be loving without first creating something to love. As Michael Reeves puts it, in his book *Delighting in the Trinity*:

> Such are the problems with nontriune gods and creation. Single-person gods, having spent eternity alone, are inevitably self-centred beings, and so it becomes hard to see why they would ever cause anything else to exist. Wouldn't the existence of a universe be an irritating distraction for the god whose greatest pleasure is looking in the mirror? ... Everything changes when it comes to the Father, Son and Spirit. Here is a God who is not essentially lonely, but who has been loving for all eternity as the Father has loved the Son in the Spirit. Loving others is not a strange or novel thing for this God at all; it is at the root of who he is.[19]

---

19 Michael Reeves, *Delighting in the Trinity: An introduction to the Christian faith* (Downers Grove, IL: IVP Academic, 2012), pp. 40–41.

When it comes to God and love, this is a common place where people often assume that the great faith traditions of the world are essentially the same. If had a pound for every time I heard somebody say, 'Every religion teaches that God is love', I could afford to buy a seaside holiday home.[20] But for all its tweetability and saccharine sentimentality, it simply isn't true.

For unlike the Bible, the Qur'an is very reticent about talking of Allah and love. In fact the main Arabic word for love, *ahabba*, is used with Allah as the subject of the verb just forty-two times and, of those occurrences, twenty-three are negative,[21] describing the kind of people Allah does *not* love. For example: 'God loves not the un-believers' (Q. 3:32); 'God loves not the prodigal' (Q. 6:141).[22] The other nineteen occurrences are conditional,[23] describing the behaviour required to earn Allah's love: 'God loves the doers of good' (Q. 3:148); 'God loves those who fight in His way, (drawn up) in lines (for battle) as if they were a solid building' (Q. 61:4).

The Qur'an simply has no conception of Allah offering anything remotely like an unconditional love to humanity. As the Pakistani scholar Daud Rahbar bluntly put it: '[T]here is not a single verse in the Qur'an that speaks of God's unconditional love for mankind . . . [Its verses] do not say that God loves all men.'[24]

Faced with this reality, some writers who are keen to create parallels between Islam and Christianity have tried to square the circle by claiming that while the Qur'an speaks little of God's love,

---

20 Admittedly probably just in Scarborough. But the point still stands.

21 See Q. 2:190, 205, 276; 3:32, 57, 140; 4:36, 107, 148; 5:64, 87; 6:141; 7:31, 55; 8:58; 16:23; 22:38; 28:76–77; 30:45; 31:18; 42:40; 57:23.

22 As Gordon Nickel points out, this is a striking contrast with Jesus' famous story in Luke 15:11–32, where the father (representing God) shows incredible love and forgiveness towards his prodigal son. See Gordon Nickel, 'The language of love in Qur'ān and Gospel', in Juan Pedro Monferrer-Sala and Angel Urban (eds.), *Sacred Text: Explorations in lexicography* (Frankfurt: Peter Lang, 2009), pp. 223–248, citing p. 229.

23 See Q. 2:195, 222 (twice); 3:31, 76, 134, 146, 148, 159; 5:13, 42, 54, 93; 9:4, 7, 108; 49:9; 60:8; 61:4.

24 Daud Rahbar, *God of Justice: A study in the ethical doctrine of the Qur'an* (Leiden: Brill, 1960), p. 225.

it often talks of God's *mercy* – and surely mercy and love are effectively the same.[25] But are they?

I live in the countryside and, because our house backs on to fields, we often get mice in our garage. After many requests from the younger members of our household, I switched to humane mouse-traps[26] and began showing mercy to our furry visitors, rather than killing them. Do I *love* mice? Not a bit of it. I may have shown mercy, but love certainly did not come into it. I suggest it is the same for Allah in the Qur'an; yes, he may be described as merciful, but this is very different from his being loving. 'Mercy' and 'love' are not interchangeable words.

Drawing out the implications of this, some Muslim scholars have gone so far as to suggest that because the Qur'an speaks so little of Allah's love, because Allah is so transcendent, and because it is crystal clear in the Qur'an that Allah is ruler and master but certainly not a father as God is described in the Bible – because of all this, Muslims should avoid using the very word 'love' in relation to Allah. The German Muslim scholar Murad Hofmann writes:

> In the Qur'an we are told that Allah is self-sufficient. This fundamental self-description definitely excludes that Allah is in love with his creation … therefore it is safer and more accurate not to speak of 'love' when addressing His clemency, compassion, benevolence, goodness, or mercy.[27]

---

25 This is a major supporting plank of Volf's thesis that Yahweh and Allah are the same: see Miroslav Volf, *Allah: A Christian response* (New York: HarperOne, 2011), ch. 8, especially pp. 153–156.

26 These allow you to trap a mouse in a small plastic tube and release it unharmed outside your house, from where it can return to the garage the following night. It's a bit like *The Great Escape*, only in reverse.

27 Murad Wilfried Hofmann, 'Differences between the Muslim and the Christian concept of divine love', in *14th General Conference of the Royal Aal al-Bayt Institute for Islamic Thought* (Amman, 2007), pp. 8–9. Discussing the verses (mentioned above) where the Qur'an does use the Arabic word for love, *aḥabba*, Hofmann suggests the word is better translated as 'likes' or 'approves' rather than 'loves'.

The God of the Bible has suffered

One of the crucial things about love is that it cannot simply be spoken about; rather, it must be demonstrated. If somebody says 'I love you' but continually insults you, throws stones at you or even just ignores you, then you might justifiably protest, 'You keep using that word, but I do not think it means what you think it means.'[28]

Love needs to be demonstrated, not just verbalized, not least because a major aspect of genuine love is that it is costly. If you truly love someone, you are willing to give of yourself to help him or her; and if the one you love is hurting, you will grieve and suffer when he or she suffers.

This brings us to the fifth and final key characteristic of Yahweh, the God of the Bible, namely that he is a God who has *experienced suffering*. Time and again we are told that Yahweh grieves over the disobedience, rebellion and brokenness of his people. For example, at the start of the story of Noah we read: 'Yahweh regretted that he had made humankind on the earth, and he was grieved in his heart' (Genesis 6:6 LEB). The Hebrew words translated 'regretted' and 'grieved' are profoundly emotional words, conveying a deep sense of sorrow.[29]

The theme of God grieving for his people runs throughout the Old Testament and is found in passage after passage, such as these words of great pathos in the book of Hosea, describing Yahweh's love for his people and grief that they have rushed headlong after other gods:

When Israel was a child, I loved him,
    and out of Egypt I called my son.
But the more I called Israel,
    the further they went from me.

---

28 With apologies to Inigo Montoya.
29 See Derek Kidner, *Genesis*, Tyndale Old Testament Commentaries (Leicester: IVP, 1967), pp. 85–86.

They sacrificed to the Baals
  and they burned incense to images . . .
How can I give you up, Ephraim?
  How can I hand you over, Israel? . . .
My heart is changed within me;
  all my compassion is aroused.
(Hosea 11:1–2, 8 NIV 1984)

Because of Yahweh's love and deep concern, he promises that he will take up our suffering, bear our wounds and carry our sorrows. In the book of Isaiah, in a famous passage that the New Testament then picks up and applies to Jesus,[30] we read:

Surely he took up our infirmities
  and carried our sorrows,
yet we considered him stricken by God,
  smitten by him, and afflicted.
But he was pierced for our transgressions,
  he was crushed for our iniquities;
the punishment that brought us peace was upon him,
  and by his wounds we are healed.
(Isaiah 53:4–5 NIV 1984)

The Bible is very clear that out of Yahweh's love for the people he has made, out of his desire for relationship with humankind, out of his intention that we should not just know *about* him but know *him* – that out of these fundamental aspects of God's character comes the plan of salvation that stands at the heart of the Bible's story. Resounding through the centuries of Old Testament history like a drumbeat comes the message that God would save his people; he would find a way to deal with our rebellion so that we could return

30 See Matthew 8:14–17; Luke 22:35–38; John 12:37–41; Acts 8:26–35; Romans 10:11–21;
  1 Peter 2:19–25.

to his presence, despite his holiness and our foolishness. That theme of God's acting to save us because we couldn't save ourselves reaches its climax in the person of Jesus, who through suffering demonstrated most clearly and concretely the very character of God:

[Jesus], being in very nature God,
    did not consider equality with God something to be grasped,
but made himself nothing,
    taking the very nature of a servant,
    being made in human likeness.
And being found in appearance as a man,
    he humbled himself
    and became obedient to death – even death on a cross!
Therefore God exalted him to the highest place
    and gave him the name that is above every name,
that at the name of Jesus every knee should bow,
    in heaven and on earth and under the earth,
and every tongue confess that Jesus Christ is Lord,
    to the glory of God the Father.
(Philippians 2:6–11 NIV 1984)

The historian and New Testament scholar Richard Bauckham explains how all the biblical themes about God and suffering come together powerfully in Jesus:

[Jesus'] humiliation belongs to the identity of God as truly as his exaltation does. The identity of God – who God is – is revealed as much in self-abasement and service as it is in exaltation and rule. The God who is high can also be low, because God is God not in seeking his own advantage but in self-giving.[31]

---

31 Richard Bauckham, *God Crucified: Monotheism and Christology in the New Testament* (Carlisle: Paternoster Press, 1998), p. 61.

So what of the Qur'an and this final theme? Does it, too, portray a God who does not just respond to our rebellion with judgment and wrath but is also moved to grief, compassion and action? In short: no. As one reads the Qur'an, it is certainly clear that human sinfulness and disobedience is a problem, that Allah gets angry about sin, but nowhere is there any hint of sadness or grief.

Consider another biblical story that the Qur'an picks up and retells, reshaping it to fit an Islamic agenda – in this case, the story of Noah and the flood, which is retold in sura 11:25–49. It opens quite differently from the Bible's version, with the Qur'an mentioning only Allah's judgment. Indeed, Noah is explicitly told not to be concerned about the fate of the disbelievers:

And Noah was inspired: 'None of your people will believe, except for the one who has (already) believed, so do not be distressed by what they have done. Build the ship under Our eyes and Our inspiration, and do not address Me concerning those who have done evil. Surely they are going to be drowned.'
(Q. 11:36–37)

Unlike the Bible, which repeatedly stresses how Yahweh grieves over his people and is moved to act for their salvation, the Qur'an takes a diametrically different angle, emphasizing that Allah is entirely unmoved and advising readers not to trouble themselves over the disbelief of unbelievers:

Do not let those who are quick to disbelieve cause you sorrow. Surely they will not harm God at all. God does not wish to assign to them any share in the Hereafter. For them (there is) a great punishment.
(Q. 3:176)

Reflecting on the Qur'an's understanding that Allah is one who is not loving or self-giving, but rather one who, by default, responds with power and anger, not ever with grief or sorrow, Muslim scholar Muhammad al-Burkawi writes:

> Allah can annihilate the universe if it seems good to Him and recreate it in an instant. He receives neither profit nor loss from whatever happens. If all the infidels became believers and all the wicked pious He would gain nothing. And if all believers became infidels it would not cause Him loss. He can annihilate even heaven itself.[32]

The heart of the difference

The question of whether or not God has experienced suffering gets right to the heart of the question of God's identity. Is God distant, remote, transcendent, impersonal and unknowable? Or is God relational, knowable, personal and loving?

The Bible and the Qur'an offer radically different descriptions of God; indeed, for most major attributes of God described by the Bible, the Qur'an either directly contradicts them or offers a radical counter-perspective. As the Australian linguist and qur'anic scholar, Mark Durie, writes: 'Once we stray beyond what is implied straightforwardly from the idea of one all-powerful creator God, the Qur'an and the Bible diverge considerably.'[33]

Do Muslims and Christians worship the same god?[34] There are many layers to that seemingly innocuous question, but at this stage

---

[32] Muhammad al-Burkawi, cited in Samuel M. Zwemer, *The Moslem Doctrine of God: An essay on the character and attributes of Allah according to the Koran and orthodox tradition* (New York: American Tract Society, 1905), p. 56.

[33] Mark Durie, *The Qur'an and Its Biblical Reflexes: Investigations into the genesis of a religion* (Lanham, MD: Lexington Books, 2018), p. 119.

[34] It is also worth noting that Yahweh, the God of the Bible, is the God worshipped by Jews as well as by Christians. Most of the first Christians were Jewish, and Christians and Jews share the Old Testament portion of the Bible. That is why in this chapter, as we

much is already clear: the Bible and the Qur'an have radically different views on the nature, character and identity of god, *and those differences make a difference.* Trying to ignore or paper over them risks grossly misrepresenting both the Qur'an and the Bible.

When we think about our first world-view question – 'Who is god?' – the Bible and the Qur'an radically disagree with each other. But what of our second question: 'Who and what are human beings?' In the next chapter, we will explore what the Bible and the Qur'an have to say on that crucial topic and see if this casts yet further light on the question of whether Christians and Muslims worship the same god.

Key takeaways

- To consider properly the question 'Do Muslims and Christians worship the same god?', it's vital that we first ask, what do you mean by the word 'god'?

- The fact of god's existence is different from the question of god's character.

- There are five key characteristics of Yahweh, the God of the Bible, that are central to his identity throughout the Old and New Testaments:
  - Yahweh is relational;
  - Yahweh (not just his commands) can be known;
  - Yahweh is holy;
  - Yahweh is love;
  - Yahweh has suffered.

(note 34 *cont.*) explored each attribute of Yahweh's character, we began with the Old Testament before then looking at how the New Testament built on that Old Testament picture. What we see between the Old Testament and the New Testament is an inheritance and continuity of themes and theology; what we see when we turn to the Qur'an is a dramatically different religious world view. In chapter 8, we'll explore what accounts for this disconnect between the Qur'an and the Bible.

- Each of those five characteristics is rejected, ignored or overwritten with an entirely different portrayal by the Qur'an as it describes Allah.

5

How much more than dust?

The Bible, the Qur'an and
what it means to be human

You can tell a great deal about individual artists from their work. Whether it is a painter or a writer, a musician or a film director, what somebody creates gives us insights into his or her character and personality. In today's digital age, where social media encourages us all to be creators, people's photo and video feeds similarly reveal much about them (in the case of many celebrity 'influencers', often their staggering lack of self-awareness).

Examining the works of particular artists can also help us avoid mixing them up or confusing them with others. For example, my friend Randy Newman is a well-known and popular American author. But he happens to share the same name as an even more popular person, a singer-songwriter, most famous for composing a song used in the 1995 film *Toy Story*. Yet, despite both men bearing the name 'Randy Newman', you would definitely be a few prawn crackers short of Set Meal B for Two if after reading *Unlikely Converts*[1] and listening to 'You've Got a Friend in Me' you continued to labour under the misconception that the same artist had created both the book and the song. (Although my friend Randy says he is occasionally tempted to accept whenever somebody calls offering him several thousand dollars to come and sing at some rich kid's birthday party.)

---

1   Randy Newman (not *that* Randy Newman), *Unlikely Converts: Improbable stories of faith* (Grand Rapids, MI: Kregel, 2019).

Just as looking at their creations can help us avoid confusing two artists with identical names, the same is true when it comes to God. As we saw in chapter 4, it is vitally important when somebody uses the word 'god' to clarify *which* god he or she is talking about, and one way of doing this is to look at what the god in question has created and how he relates to what he has made.

Playthings of the gods

Let me illustrate what I mean by first taking an example from long ago: the god Marduk, who features in the creation myth of ancient Babylon, the Enuma Elish. In that very early story, we read how Marduk first creates the world out of the dead bits of other gods he has killed, in a kind of celestial version of a Body Worlds show:[2]

> After the warrior Marduk had bound and slain his
>   enemies . . .
> He strengthened his hold on the Bound Gods,
> And returned to [the goddess] Tia-mat, whom he had bound,
> [He] placed his feet on the lower parts of Tia-mat
> And with his merciless club smashed her skull.
> He severed her arteries
> And let the North wind bear up (her blood) to give the news . . .
> He split her in two like a dried fish:
> One half of her he set up and stretched out as the heavens . . .
> From her two eyes he let the Euphrates and Tigris flow . . .
> [The other half of her] he stretched out and made it firm
>   as the earth.[3]

---

2 Body Worlds is a travelling exhibition of dissected human bodies, created by the German anatomist Gunther von Hagens. Over 18,000 people have donated their bodies after death to the exhibition, a strange community of the deceased united in one might call an *esprit de corpse*.

3 Enuma Elish, IV:123 – V:62, <www.ancient.eu/article/225/enuma-elish---the-babylonian-epic-of-creation---fu>.

After creating the heavens and the earth, Marduk is then approached by the other gods, who complain about the hard work that looking after creation is going to be for them. 'No problem,' says Marduk cheerfully and, using the blood of another dead deity, creates the first humans, tasking them with being slaves to the gods:

> When Marduk heard the gods' speech
> He conceived a desire to accomplish clever things.
> He opened his mouth addressing Ea,
> He counsels that which he had pondered in his heart,
> 'I will bring together blood to form bone,
> I will bring into being Lullû, whose name shall be "man".
> I will create Lullû – man
> On whom the toil of the gods will be laid that they may rest.'[4]

Aside from this reading like the kind of creation account that the horror writer Stephen King might have dreamt up after a bout of insomnia and too many helpings of Roquefort, the implications that follow from this story are pretty clear: rather than one all-powerful god who is the source of all that exists, we have a bunch of minor godlets at war with one another; creation is not so much a careful, deliberate choice as an explosion in an abattoir; and human beings have no special status or value, but are simply the playthings of the gods, toiling away so that Marduk and his mates can have a lie-in of a morning. A creation story like this tells us a very good deal about the kind of gods behind it, and it is not a pretty picture.

Creation out of nothing

Thankfully, the Enuma Elish is light years away from the Bible and the Qur'an, both of which are adamant that the one true God created

---

4   Enuma Elish, VI:1–8, source as above.

all that exists, the entire of reality, literally from nothing. Before God's creative act there wasn't the debris of a cosmic battle with bits of dead gods lying untidily around the place, but literally nothing: *no-thing*. The Bible puts it like this:

> In the beginning was the Word, and the Word was with God, and the Word was God. He was with God in the beginning. Through him all things were made; without him nothing was made that has been made.
> (John 1:1–3)

While the Qur'an states: '[Allah is the] Originator of the heavens and the earth. When He decrees something, He simply says to it, "Be!" and it is' (Q. 2:117).

That God is the source of all that is, the ultimate 'it' behind all reality, the one who called into existence every particle and who wrote every law of physics – that God is the sole creator is something on which Muslims and Christians can wholeheartedly agree, a not unimportant point of contact between these two faith traditions.

Furthermore, both the Bible and the Qur'an repeatedly make the point that I made at the start of this chapter about artists and their works, namely that if you want to know what God is like, take a look at his creation. For example, the Bible proclaims:

> The heavens declare the glory of God;
> the skies proclaim the work of his hands.
> Day after day they pour forth speech;
> night after night they display knowledge.
> There is no speech or language
> where their voice is not heard.
> Their voice goes out into all the earth,
> their words to the ends of the world.
> (Psalm 19:1–4 NIV 1984)

In other words, if you want to begin to know what God is like, listen to the 'song' that creation in all of its splendour is metaphorically singing. A similar theme can be found in the Qur'an:

Those are the signs of the Book. What has been sent down to you from your Lord is the truth, but most of the people do not believe.

(It is) God who raised up the heavens without pillars that you (can) see. Then He mounted the throne, and subjected the sun and the moon, each one running (its course) for an appointed time. He directs the (whole) affair. He makes the signs distinct, so that you may be certain of the meeting with your Lord.

He (it is) who stretched out the earth, and placed on it firm mountains and rivers. And of all the fruits He has placed on it two in pairs. He covers the day with the night. Surely in that are signs indeed for a people who reflect.

(Q. 13:1–3)

Making a similar argument to that made by the Bible in places like the book of Romans,[5] the Qur'an here suggests that even if people ignore what Allah has said in the book he has revealed, they are still without excuse because creation itself is a sign about what Allah is like.

The pinnacle of creation

When it comes to learning about the character, nature and identity of an artist or creator, you can certainly discover some things by looking at their minor works, but you will learn much more by carefully

5 'Since the creation of the world God's invisible qualities – his eternal power and divine nature – have been clearly seen, being understood from what has been made, so that people are without excuse' (Romans 1:20).

studying an artist's greatest work, their most significant creation, their magnum opus. For example, if you want to find out what J. R. R. Tolkien was like, it would be better to carefully read *The Lord of the Rings*, not just dip into one of his short novels like *Roverandom*. If you want to understand George Frederick Handel, you will make far more progress by familiarizing yourself with *Messiah* than merely listening to his little-known operatic work *Alceste*.

Much the same is true when it comes to God and his creative works. For sure, the heavens and the earth, the sun and the moon, the mountains and rivers and so forth can provide *some* information about the god who made them, but if we want to get a deeper insight into God's identity, it is to the pinnacle of creation that we must look. The Bible repeatedly explains that the crowning achievement of Yahweh's work of creation was humankind:

What is mankind that you are mindful of them,
    human beings that you care for them?
You have made them a little lower than the angels
    and crowned them with glory and honour.
(Psalm 8:4–5)

That human beings are unique and set apart is something that every-body instinctively recognizes, whether a person has a religious faith or not. I recall taking part in a debate at the University of Hull a few years ago with Andrew Copson, the head of what was then called the British Humanist Association (now Humanists UK). During the debate, I kept pressing Andrew on why, as an ardent secularist, he seemed to think human beings were special – he had repeatedly mentioned human value, human dignity, human moral responsibility, and so forth. He finally admitted that even as a non-religious person, he could not easily escape the idea of human uniqueness.[6]

---

6 See also the discussion in Andy Steiger, *Reclaimed: How Jesus restores our humanity in a dehumanized world* (Grand Rapids, MI: Zondervan, 2020), pp. 45–63.

All of this connects to the second of our four world-view questions: 'Who and what are human beings?' It is almost impossible to overstate how important this question is; it arguably lies behind every major ethical, cultural and political debate of our age. So, if the Bible and the Qur'an agree that human beings are the pinnacle of God's creation, and if it were the case that Allah, the God of the Qur'an, and Yahweh, the God of the Bible, were the same, then surely we would expect a very similar answer to the question 'What does it mean to be human?' when we carefully study the Qur'an and the Bible. So what do our two texts have to tell us?

The Bible and what it means to be human

At the heart of the Bible's understanding of what it means to be a human being lies a remarkable claim. The book of Genesis tells us that human beings were made from 'the dust of the ground',[7] but the Bible makes it clear that this is not what a human being *is*. In just the same way that one cannot reduce the *Mona Lisa* to the chemical constituents from which its paint is made, or the plays of Shakespeare to merely the individual letters with which they are written, one cannot reduce *us* to just the bits from which we are made. There is a fundamental difference between what something is made of and what something is.

In its very first chapter of its very first book, the Bible sets out what it means to be a human:

Then God said, 'Let us make mankind in our image, in our likeness, so that they may rule over the fish in the sea and the birds in the sky, over the livestock and all the wild animals, and over all the creatures that move along the ground.'

7 Genesis 2:7.

So God created mankind in his own image,
in the image of God he created them;
male and female he created them.
(Genesis 1:26–27)

There are a number of interesting things to notice here. The first is that bearing the image of God is not something towards which humans must strive, something they must aspire to or seek to earn. Rather, our status as 'image bearers' is something given to us as a gift right at the beginning: it is intrinsic to the very nature of a human being. As Old Testament scholar John Walton puts it:

This view is different from both the ancient Near East and different from modern materialism. In the ancient Near East people were created as slaves to the gods. The world was created by the gods for the gods, and people met the needs of the gods. In the Bible, God has no needs, and his cosmic temple [creation] has been created for people whom he desires to be in relationship with him. In modern materialism people are nothing but physical forms having no function other than to survive. The theology of Genesis 1 is crucial to a right understanding of our identity and place in the world.[8]

Second, notice how the Bible is very careful to include the *whole* of humanity in its description. In stark contrast to many ancient (and some worryingly more contemporary) world views that denigrate one half of the human race by assigning a special value or privilege to men, the Bible is crystal clear: being an image bearer is a status carried by both men and women – it goes along with being part of the human race, not simply some small subset of it.

---

8   John H. Walton, *The Lost World of Genesis One: Ancient cosmology and the origins debate* (Downers Grove, IL: IVP, 2009), p. 148.

That human beings bear the image of God is not some peripheral theological idea; it is absolutely central to the Bible's understanding of who human beings are and it flows very naturally out of the Bible's understanding of who God is. Not least, it suggests that because we have been made in the image of a God who is relational and personal, we too are relational and personal. Theologian Michael Reeves explains:

> That we are made in the image of God could and does mean many things; but the fact that the God in whose image we are made is specifically the triune God of love has repercussions that echo all through Scripture. Made in the image of this God, we are created to delight in harmonious relationship, to love God, to love each other.[9]

Later in the book of Genesis, the Bible returns to the idea of human beings as image bearers, appealing to it as the foundation of morality and ethics. Why is human life sacred? Why is it that murder and violence are *wrong*? The Bible answers this in terms of the image of God: 'As for the one shedding the blood of humankind, by humankind his blood shall be shed, for God made humankind in his own image' (Genesis 9:6 LEB).

Historically, the idea that human beings bear the image of God has had a tremendous impact. Beginning in the fifteenth century, a group of jurists and theologians, deeply concerned about how Spanish and other European colonists were mistreating natives in the lands they had conquered, began unpacking the implications of what it meant that *all* people bore God's image. In 1610, the Spanish Jesuit priest and philosopher, Francisco Suárez, published an incredibly influential essay, *On the Laws*, which argued that all humans have rights because

---

9 Michael Reeves, *Delighting in the Trinity: An introduction to the Christian faith* (Downers Grove, IL: IVP Academic, 2012), pp. 64–65.

they were created in God's image.[10] His essay influenced John Locke, often considered to be the father of modern democracy, who in turn influenced Thomas Jefferson, who wrote this idea right into the heart of the American Declaration of Independence, with its powerful proclamation that all are created equal, 'endowed by their Creator with certain unalienable Rights, [and] that among these are Life, Liberty, and the Pursuit of Happiness'.[11] From there, the idea flowed onwards and eventually influenced the Universal Declaration of Human Rights, published by the United Nations General Assembly in 1948.[12]

Modern human rights theory did not develop in a vacuum; rather, its thinkers were deeply rooted (whether they realized it or not) in the Bible's idea that human beings bear the image of God, which is itself derived from the Bible's idea that the God in whose image we are made is relational, personal, knowable and loving. As the celebrated French atheist philosopher, Luc Ferry, writes:

> In direct contradiction [to the Greek world], Christianity was to introduce the notion that humanity was fundamentally identical, that men were equal in dignity – an unprecedented idea at the time, and one to which our world owes its entire democratic inheritance. But this notion of equality did not come from nowhere.[13]

The biblical theme that human beings are image bearers, so foundational for human rights, begins in Genesis but flows on throughout the whole of the Bible to where it culminates in the New Testament. There, as we have seen, we encounter the person of Jesus – who, it is

---

10 See Thomas E. Woods, *How the Catholic Church Built Western Civilization* (Washington, DC: Regnery, 2005), pp. 133–150.

11 See 'Text of the Declaration of Independence', 4 July 1776, Harvard University Declaration Resources Project, <https://declaration.fas.harvard.edu/resources/text>.

12 See 'Universal Declaration of Human Rights', 10 December 1948, United Nations, <www.un.org/en/universal-declaration-human-rights/index.html>.

13 Luc Ferry, *A Brief History of Thought: A philosophical guide to living* (New York: Harper Perennial, 2011 [2010]), p. 72.

claimed, is not simply another religious leader, but God-in-the-flesh, come to reveal not just what God is like but also what human beings were intended to be, *image bearers*: 'The Son is the *image* of the invisible God' (Colossians 1:15).

In other words, says the Bible, if you want to understand why human beings are the way they are – personal, relational, creative, moral and so forth – you must look to the God whose image they bear. And if you want to understand what that image looks like in all its fullness, look to Jesus.

The Qur'an and what it means to be human

When we turn to the Qur'an to explore its answer to the question of what it means to be human, we can note right at the start that, as we saw before, the Qur'an retells the story of the first humans, Adam and Eve. But rather than start where Genesis begins, with the actual creation of Adam and Eve, the Qur'an starts slightly further back, reflecting an ancient Jewish legend about an event that happened just before God made human beings.[14] According to this tradition, God first explained his intention to the angels, who promptly began to protest. The Qur'an's version of the story is found in several places, including in sura 2:

> (Remember) when your Lord said to the angels, 'Surely I am placing on the earth a ruler.' They said, 'Will You place on it someone who will foment corruption on it, and shed blood, while we glorify (You) with Your praise and call You holy?' He said, 'Surely I know what you do not know.'
> (Q. 2:30)

---

14 One Jewish version of this story can be found in the Babylonian Talmud, *Tractate Sanhedrin* 38b (fifth or sixth century AD). It is quoted and discussed in Gabriel Said Reynolds, *The Qur'ān and the Bible: Text and commentary* (New Haven, CT: Yale University Press, 2018), pp. 35–36.

Whenever the Qur'an retells biblical stories and traditions, it adjusts and adapts them, reshaping them to fit its own theology and agenda. We see this here in this verse where the biblical idea of image bearing has been quietly dropped and instead the Qur'an has focused on the idea of humanity's status as a *ruler* over the rest of creation. That concept was certainly there in Genesis, but it was a preamble to the much bigger idea of image bearing – an idea that the Qur'an ignores entirely.

The word translated into English here as 'ruler' is the Arabic word *khalīfa*, and while it certainly contains the idea of authority and ruling over,[15] the root idea behind the term is also that of succeeding or following – an idea that possibly helps makes better sense of Q. 2:30. For a natural question that occurs when one reads this verse is why the angels were so negative. Did they have amazing powers of foresight? Were they just of a naturally and curmudgeonly disposition, perhaps worried that human beings would compete with them for first place in the coffee queue of a morning? When we turn to the later Islamic tradition that developed after the Qur'an, early Muslim scholars answered this question by telling the story of how, long before human beings had come on the scene, Allah had made another species, the jinn, who had rebelled and caused all manner of chaos. According to one of the earliest commentators on the Qur'an, Muhammad's cousin Ibn Abbas (d. 687):

> The first to live on earth were the jinn, and they corrupted it and shed blood, and some killed some others . . . God sent Iblīs against them with an army of angels. And Iblīs and those who were with him killed them until he surrounded them on islands in the seas and the tops of mountains . . . Then God said to the angels who were with him, 'I am about to create on earth a vicegerent (*khalīfa*).'[16]

---

15 See also Q. 6:165; 7:69, 74; 10:14, 73; 27:62; 35:39; 38:2.
16 Cited in Al-Tabari (d. AD 923), *Tafsir al-Tabari*, 1.201 (vol. 1). See Whitney S. Bodman, *The Poetics of Iblis: Narrative theology in the Qur'ān* (Cambridge, MA: Harvard University Press, 2011), p. 121.

Whether or not the Qur'an's idea of humans being *khalīfa* is intended to convey more the idea of succession (coming after the jinn) or more the idea of ruling over, one thing is very clear: it does not imply representation or image bearing, or anything remotely similar. Islamic theology has always been very clear that Allah is utterly other; no human being, neither individual nor corporately, could represent him.

Although the Qur'an reports that angels would not trust human beings as far as they could throw them (and being angels, that's probably pretty far), the Qur'an does go on to make quite positive statements about humanity. For example, it stresses that humans are not just material but have a spiritual component to them as well:

> [Allah] brought about the creation of the human from clay; then He made his progeny from an extract of despicable water; then He fashioned him and breathed into him some of His spirit, and made for you hearing and sight and hearts. Little thanks you show!
> (Q. 32:7–9)

The Qur'an also teaches that human beings are honoured and distinguished above the rest of creation: 'Certainly We [Allah] have honored the sons of Adam, and carried them on the shore and the sea, and provided them with good things, and favored them greatly over many of those whom We have created' (Q. 17:70).

For the Qur'an, human beings have an elevated status, yes, but they certainly are not made in God's image and there is certainly not the slightest hint of any idea that human beings could ever call God 'Father', or be considered in any way children of God. Indeed, the main image that the Qur'an uses to describe the relationship between Allah and a human being is that of master and slave: '[Allah] is the Omnipotent over His slaves, and He is the Wise, the Knower' (Q. 6:18).[17]

---

17 The Arabic word *'abd* ('slave') is used over a hundred times in the Qur'an to describe human beings.

Interestingly, although the Qur'an never once repeats the ancient biblical idea that human beings bear the image of God, later Islamic theologians and tradition tellers, interacting with Jews and Christians as the Islamic empire expanded, came across the biblical language of 'image' and, not knowing quite what to do with it, wove stories and legends around it that took it in some very strange directions. In the hadith, the collection of traditions about Muhammad's life and teachings, we read:

> Narrated Abu Huraira: The Prophet [Muhammad] said, 'Allah created Adam in His [image], sixty cubits (about 30 meters) in height' ... The Prophet added 'So whoever will enter Paradise, will be of the shape and picture of Adam. Since then the creation of Adam's (offspring) ... is being diminished ... to the present time.'[18]

The legend of Adam's tremendous height is well known in many Muslim contexts and occasionally surfaces in the media. For example, back in 2004, the Bangladeshi news website, *The New Nation*, fell for a prank in which somebody had doctored a photo of an archaeological dig and made it appear as if a gigantic ancient skeleton had been unearthed by scientists from the sands of the Arabian Empty Quarter.[19]

The loss in the Qur'an and the Islamic traditions of the concept and meaning of humanity bearing God's image has some major implications because so much stands on this idea, most significantly the whole edifice of human rights and the passionate insistence that every person – no matter his or her race, gender, religion or background – has inherent value and dignity. It is noteworthy that after

---

18 See Sahih al-Bukhari 6227.

19 Saalim Alvi, 'Giant human skeleton found in Saudi Arabia', *The New Nation*, 22 April 2004. See also James Owen, '"Skeleton of giant" is internet photo hoax', *National Geographic*, 13 December 2007, <www.nationalgeographic.com/news/2007/12/skeleton-giant-photo-hoax>.

the Universal Declaration of Human Rights (UDHR) was proclaimed in 1948, there were several attempts by groups of Muslim countries to come up with alternative statements. Perhaps the most famous is the Cairo Declaration on Human Rights in Islam, published by the nations who make up the Organisation of Islamic Cooperation. It adopts much of the language of the UDHR but weakens it in significant ways – for example, failing to protect freedom of religion (especially the freedom to convert) and stating repeatedly that rights and freedoms are all subject to Islamic sharia law. Given that some interpretations of sharia law condone treating women as if they bear second-class status and that most schools of sharia law also consider apostasy from Islam to warrant the death penalty, this is deeply problematic.

Ideas have consequences

The story is told of a country farmer, leaning over a field gate beside a lane, somewhere deep in rural England far from the madding crowd, chewing contemplatively on a blade of grass and enjoying the summer sunshine. In the distance comes the sound of an engine, and in due course a large, expensive German car[20] pulls up. The driver winds down the window and a cultured voice booms out: 'Excuse me, my hardy fellow, but could you tell me the way to Exonbury?' The farmer scratches his beard and thinks long and hard. Then he announces sagely: 'Well, sir, if I was heading for Exonbury, I wouldn't start from here.'

Where you start from is very important, whether you are navigating, or wrestling with a crucial question like 'What does it mean to be human?' As we have seen, the Bible and the Qur'an have fundamentally different answers to that question. For the Qur'an, humans are valuable and important, but just slaves of Allah. For the

---

20 'Expensive German car' being, of course, a tautology.

Bible, humans are far more than that: they are image bearers, people with intrinsic and fundamental value and dignity because of their very nature. As those two ideas have played themselves out in history, quite different systems of justice, culture and civilization have grown from their foundations.

The Qur'an and the Bible, when they present these very different views of what it means to be human, also tell us a great deal about Allah, the God of the Qur'an, and Yahweh, the God of the Bible – and as they do, caution us about too quickly confusing or equating them. Just as different human artists often create very different works (only a fool would confuse the writings of Jane Austen and those of Stephen King, for instance[21]), so very-different-looking gods create very-different-looking human beings and those differences have tremendous consequences. *Who* you believe God is directly affects *what* you believe human beings are.

Do Muslims and Christians worship the same god? So far we have seen how the Qur'an and the Bible's answers to our first two world-view questions ('What is God like?' and 'What are human beings?') are fundamentally different, suggesting that rather than casually assume that just because Muslims and Christians both use the word 'god' they mean the *same* god, we need to look deeper. In the next chapter we will turn to our third world-view question – 'What's gone wrong with the world?' – to see whether the gap that has opened up between Allah and Yahweh begins to narrow, or whether the gap will turn into a chasm.

Key takeaways

- Just as studying the works of an artist, writer or musician can tell you a lot about the person, so looking at what the Bible or Qur'an says that God has made can tell us much about Yahweh

---

21 Although the makers of the film *Pride and Prejudice and Zombies* (2016) certainly gave it a try.

and Allah. This is especially true when we look at what the Bible and Qur'an both agree is the pinnacle of God's creative work, namely the human species.

- The Bible teaches that human beings are made in God's image, created to enjoy relationship with him and to reflect something of his nature to the rest of creation. The dignity that flows from humans being image bearers laid the foundation for the modern concept of human rights.

- The Qur'an teaches that human beings have an elevated status, but are not in any sense made in God's image. For the Qur'an, the primary image for the relationship that exists between Allah and human beings is not that of father and children but of master and servants.

6

The crack in everything
What in the world is wrong with the world?

I have a confession to make. I am a science fiction and fantasy fan. There, I've admitted it. I have shelves full of everything from Asimov to Wells, a digital media library full of *Star Trek* episodes, and pieces of geeky paraphernalia dotted around my study, including a statuette of the Librarian from Terry Pratchett's Discworld perched on my desk.[1]

But the sci-fi show I love the most is unquestionably *Doctor Who*, which holds the world record for the longest-running science fiction serial. The show tells the story of a mysterious figure known simply as the Doctor, last of the Time Lords. Travelling through space and time in a battered blue police box,[2] the Doctor has adventures involving fearsome enemies, scary monsters and a whole lot of running down corridors.

In the 2010 season of *Doctor Who*, the story arc is built around the mystery of the ominous glowing cracks that keep appearing in walls wherever the Doctor turns up. Eventually it is revealed that the entirety of time and space had been shattered when the Doctor's time machine, the TARDIS, blew up, causing a crack in the very fabric of reality itself.

By now, this is probably way too much geekery and has undoubtedly left many readers needing a sit-down, or at least a dose of Jane Austen (which in my view suffers badly from a lack of robots

---

1   The Librarian is an orangutan (obviously).
2   Don't ask. (Those two little words helpfully explain the majority of science fiction concepts.)

and explosions[3]). But whether one is a sci-fi fan or not, the idea of there being a crack in everything is fascinating, for it does not take a rocket scientist, or any kind of genius, or even a Time Lord to notice that the world in which we live, the *real* world, is pretty badly broken. It too is cracked – and for far more serious reasons than a fictional blue box going bang.

Big cracks and little ones

The real world is very obviously broken in some rather major ways. One could point to widespread poverty and deprivation, or racism and discrimination, violence and war. Or to issues like environmental degradation and pollution, famine and disease, and so on – the list goes on and on like a particularly depressing final credits roll at the end of an awfully nihilistic movie.

But as well as the big cracks, there are smaller ones too, a network of fractures like those in a plate dropped on the floor by a careless toddler. These cracks show up in all the *little* ways in which we go wrong as human beings: selfishness and pride, pettiness and self-superiority, arrogance and vindictiveness – all the everyday nastinesses of which you and I are all too capable. And the small cracks and the big cracks are connected. Consider these sobering words from Gus Speth, an environmental scientist and former Dean of the School of Forestry and Environmental Studies at Yale University:

> I used to think that the top environmental problems were biodiversity loss, ecosystem collapse, and climate change. I thought that thirty years of good science could address these problems. I was wrong. The top environmental problems are *selfishness, greed, and apathy,* and to deal with these we need a

---

3   Except in 'Beyond a Joke', episode 6 of *Red Dwarf* VII (1997).

cultural and spiritual transformation. And we scientists don't know how to do that.[4]

This is sobering because one of the things about the *big* cracks in our world is that it is easy to point at them and shriek (or festoon our social media posts with hashtags), but not actually have to *do* anything. After all, I can't personally remove all the plastic from the oceans, solve structural injustices or reduce global poverty, so instead I just feel #VeryAngry and then move on. But eventually we cannot escape the fact that the bigger and the smaller cracks join up and that part of what's wrong with the world is *me*. As the award-winning writer Francis Spufford puts it:

> [L]ike all bad news [this] is not very welcome, especially if you let yourself take seriously the implication that we actually *want* the destructive things we do, that they are not just an accident that keeps happening to poor little us, but part of our nature; that we are truly cruel as well as truly tender, truly loving and at the same time truly likely to take a quick nasty pleasure in wasting or breaking love, scorching it knowingly up as the fuel for some hotter or more exciting feeling.[5]

All of us know, deep down, that the world is broken, and the wiser, more reflective or simply more battle-scarred and weary among us realize that the cracks involve us. But what, *precisely*, has gone wrong? The plate is broken on the kitchen floor, but was it my five-year-old son, the family cat or an earth tremor?

---

4 Cited in Daniel Crockett, 'Nature connection will be the next big human trend', *Huffington Post*, 22 August 2014, <www.huffingtonpost.co.uk/daniel-crockett/nature-connection-will-be-the-next-big-human-trend_b_5698267.html>; my emphasis.

5 Francis Spufford, *Unapologetic: Why, despite everything, Christianity can still make surprising emotional sense* (London: Faber & Faber, 2013 [2012]), pp. 29–30.

Different diagnoses

Why the world is so badly broken is one of the major questions that the world's religions try to answer. As Stephen Prothero points out in his book *God Is Not One*, each of the world's religions articulates a problem ('What's wrong with the world?'), a solution ('How do we fix the problem?') and some kind of method ('What's the path from problem to solution?').[6] Now if (and I stress *if*) Islam and Christianity are very closely related, in particular if it is the same god behind both of them, then presumably we should see them draw very similar conclusions about what has gone wrong with the world. After all, how somebody diagnoses a problem is a significant clue to his or her identity.

Some years back, I had a friend who worked for a large company in London. The team that he was part of had the misfortune to be supervised by not one but two managers – an example of a new, exciting and innovative business tool called 'Matrix management'.[7] Both managers thought the team was riven with problems, but they disagreed profoundly about the cause of those problems. One manager thought the team had *too much* conflict in it and so he was always trying to bring harmony and unity; the other thought there wasn't *enough* conflict and so she was always trying to stir things up. You could never confuse one manager with the other: if an unsigned memo turned up with some proposal to solve the team's internal difficulties, you could instantly guess which leader had proposed it, depending on whether the suggested solution involved cushions and safe places, or team-building exercises using projectile weapons.

I want to suggest that it is the same when it comes to Allah and Yahweh. Yes, both Islam and Christianity think that the world is

---

6   Stephen Prothero, *God Is Not One: The eight rival religions that run the world* (New York: HarperOne, 2010), p. 14.

7   Presumably so-called because employees struggling under Matrix management feel like they're part of a dystopian world where nothing is really what it seems.

cracked; they have that in common not just with each other but with every religion, philosophy and political outlook. But when it comes to the *root* of the problem, the *cause* of the cracks, the Bible and the Qur'an have entirely different diagnoses, deriving from their very different understandings of who god is.

The Bible: the problem of separation

At the heart of the Bible's diagnosis of what has gone wrong with the world is the condition that it calls 'sin' – a word used to translate over a dozen different Hebrew and Greek words that occur over 2,000 times in the Bible. 'Sin' is arguably one of the most misunderstood terms in our modern world, where it is too often associated with only the most heinous of offences (murder, robbery, folk music appreciation) or else is viewed as terribly Victorian, a monochromatic word wreathed in cobwebs, a linguistic ghost of a long-dead culture that disapproved of anything that looked even remotely like fun.

But behind the idea of 'sin' in the Bible lies something much deeper, and it is best seen by quoting at length one of the Bible's most famous stories, the fall of Adam and Eve, found in the book of Genesis:

Now the serpent was more crafty than any other wild animal which Yahweh God had made. He said to the woman, 'Did God indeed say, "You shall not eat from any tree in the garden"?' The woman said to the serpent, 'From the fruit of the trees of the garden we may eat, but from the fruit of the tree that is in the midst of the garden, God said, "You shall not eat from it, nor shall you touch it, lest you die".' But the serpent said to the woman, 'You shall not surely die. For God knows that on the day you both eat from it, then your eyes will be opened and you both shall be like gods, knowing good and evil.' When the woman saw that the tree was good for food and that it was a

93

delight to the eyes, and the tree was desirable to make one wise, then she took from its fruit and she ate. And she gave it also to her husband with her, and he ate. Then the eyes of both of them were opened, and they knew that they were naked. And they sewed together fig leaves and they made for themselves coverings.

Then they heard the sound of Yahweh God walking in the garden at the windy time of day. And the man and his wife hid themselves from the presence of Yahweh God among the trees of the garden. And Yahweh God called to the man and said to him, 'Where are you?' And he replied, 'I heard the sound of you in the garden, and I was afraid because I am naked, so I hid myself.' Then he asked, 'Who told you that you were naked? Have you eaten from the tree from which I forbade you to eat?' And the man replied, 'The woman whom you gave to be with me – she gave to me from the tree and I ate.' Then Yahweh God said to the woman, 'What is this you have done?' And the woman said, 'The serpent deceived me, and I ate.' Then Yahweh God said to the serpent,

'Because you have done this,
 you will be cursed
 more than any domesticated animal
 and more than any wild animal.
On your belly you shall go
 and dust you shall eat
 all the days of your life.
And I will put hostility
 between you and between the woman,
 and between your offspring and between her offspring;
he will strike you on the head,
 and you will strike him on the heel.'
(Genesis 3:1–15 LEB)

The story is fascinating, especially for what it reveals about the nature of Adam and Eve's sin. For lying behind their desire to determine good and evil for themselves was apparently an even deeper temptation, namely the desire to become like God. Satan, in the form of the serpent, appeals to that idea directly. This is a theme that runs onwards through the Bible, which repeatedly returns to the idea that our basic problem is we want to replace God, either with something else or with *us* – for sometimes we simply want to be God ourselves.

Furthermore, through this foundational story in Genesis about what has gone wrong with creation, we also see the idea that sin involves something much deeper than just commandment-breaking. Yes, Yahweh is holy and desires moral purity; however, he wants this not simply for its own sake but because he seeks relationship with humanity. Notice how in the middle of the story God is found walking and talking in the garden with Adam and Eve. And in that relational context, one reason for the commandment not to eat the fruit of the tree (the sole instruction the first human couple were given) was not because there was something magical about the tree, but because the underlying question was whether they were willing to trust God.

In the Bible, the God who is relational, the God who can be known, the God who is love reveals his identity through forming covenant commitments with human beings. The concept of covenant, of God and humanity committing themselves deeply to each other, is one of the central themes of the whole of the Bible. Yahweh has committed himself to human beings in love and faithfulness, and in return asks the same of humanity, commandment-keeping being one way that commitment is shown: 'Lord, the great and awesome God, who keeps his covenant of love with those who love him and keep his commandments' (Daniel 9:4).

Perhaps the closest analogy to the depth of commitment that lies behind a covenant would be marriage, for that too is a relationship involving love and commitment, promises and faithfulness, and boundaries to protect it. Therefore it is not entirely surprising that the metaphor the Bible most commonly reaches for to describe humanity's sin and rebellion is adultery. This is illustrated most powerful and poignantly in the book of Hosea, where the eponymous prophet is told by Yahweh to marry an unfaithful woman so that Hosea's marriage will be a prophetic sign of how Israel has behaved towards Yahweh:

> At the beginning when Yahweh spoke through Hosea,
> Yahweh said to Hosea,
>> 'Go, take for yourself a wife and children of whoredom,
>> because the land commits great whoredom
>>> forsaking Yahweh.'
> (Hosea 1:2 LEB)

Just as unfaithfulness tears apart a marriage, so sin and the human tendency to replace God as the first love in our hearts with other things has shattered the covenant relationship between humanity and God. Time and again, as we move through two thousand years of biblical history, the Bible makes it clear that the problem is far deeper than just our breaking of God's laws, because simple law-keeping cannot change minds, let alone hearts. Even when the whole of the Old Testament is reduced to just two commandments, as was done by Jesus, we still end up falling short:

> Hearing that Jesus had silenced the Sadducees, the Pharisees got together. One of them, an expert in the law, tested him with this question: 'Teacher, which is the greatest commandment in the Law?'
> Jesus replied: '"Love the Lord your God with all your heart and with all your soul and with all your mind." This is the first and greatest commandment. And the second is like it: "Love

your neighbour as yourself." All the Law and the Prophets hang on these two commandments.'
(Matthew 22:34–40)

What's gone wrong with the world, according to the Bible? Simply that the choice that Adam and Eve made back at the beginning, to turn from a close relationship with God by attempting to make themselves the centre of the story, has had consequences right down through history. Sin has spread like a cancer throughout creation and thus we fail to love God and we fail to love our neighbour. Each of us simply repeats the same pattern seen in the fall of Adam and Eve, with the result that humans are separated from God and estranged from one another: 'All have sinned and fall short of the glory of God' (Romans 3:23).

For the Bible, the basic problem is that human beings are unfaithful and have broken the relationship they were designed to have with God. Everything else that has gone wrong – the ribbon of cracks that has spread out through reality – can be traced back to that initial fracture. The world is not merely cracked, but our very nature has been corrupted too; as King David writes in one of the Bible's most poignant psalms:

I know my transgressions,
    and my sin is always before me.
Against you, you only, have I sinned
    and done what is evil in your sight;
so you are right in your verdict
    and justified when you judge.
Surely I was sinful at birth,
    sinful from the time my mother conceived me.
(Psalm 51:3–5)

But despite this terrible predicament that humans find themselves in, all is not bleak pessimism, for resounding through the Bible like a distant drumbeat is the great promise that one day our relationship with God will be restored and our nature put right. One day, the Bible declares, there will be a new covenant, written not on tablets of stone (like the Ten Commandments) but in hearts and minds:

> 'This is the covenant that I will make with the house of Israel after those days,' declares Yahweh: 'I will put my law in their inward parts and on their hearts I will write it, and I will be to them God, and they themselves will be to me people. And they will no longer teach each one his neighbor, or each one his brother, saying "Know Yahweh," for all of them will know me, from their smallest and up to their greatest,' declares Yahweh, 'for I will forgive their iniquity and their sin I will no longer remember.'
> (Jeremiah 31:33–34 LEB)

The Qur'an: the problem of forgetfulness

When we turn to the Qur'an and ask what Allah, the God of the Qur'an, thinks has gone wrong with the world, we soon notice that the Qur'an also speaks a lot about sin. Several different Arabic words are used to express the concept of sin in the roughly one hundred times in the Qur'an it is mentioned (significantly fewer than the two thousand or so times the Bible talks about sin, even when one adjusts for the much shorter length of the Qur'an).[8]

Fascinatingly, when it comes to the question of human sinfulness, the Qur'an tells the same foundational story as the Bible, drawing both on the Bible and on early Jewish and Christian traditions as it

---

8 Depending on precisely how one handles certain word-divisions, the Qur'an contains 77,429 words while the Bible contains 558,299 words. Many of these statistics were produced by medieval Jewish, Christian and Islamic scholars whose labours – long before computers were invented and made this kind of stuff easier – are an impressive illustration of the power of an enquiring mind plus insomnia.

retells the story of Adam and his wife (who is unnamed in the Qur'an):[9]

'O Adam! dwell thou and thy wife in the Garden, and enjoy (its good things) as ye wish: but approach not this tree, or ye run into harm and transgression.'

Then began Satan to whisper suggestions to them, bringing openly before their minds all their shame that was hidden from them (before): he said: 'Your Lord only forbade you this tree, lest ye should become angels or such beings as live for ever.'

And he swore to them both, that he was their sincere adviser.

So by deceit he brought about their fall: when they tasted of the tree, their shame became manifest to them, and they began to sew together the leaves of the garden over their bodies. And their Lord called unto them: 'Did I not forbid you that tree, and tell you that Satan was an avowed enemy unto you?'

They said: 'Our Lord! We have wronged our own souls: If thou forgive us not and bestow not upon us Thy Mercy, we shall certainly be lost.'

(Allah) said: 'Get ye down. With enmity between your-selves. On earth will be your dwelling-place and your means of livelihood – for a time.'

He said: 'Therein shall ye live, and therein shall ye die; but from it shall ye be taken out (at last).'

(Q. 7:19–25)

Given that the Qur'an tells the very same origin story as the Bible, does this mean that it offers an identical diagnosis concerning what

---

9   As well as the Bible, the Qur'an also draws on traditions from the Jewish text *The Life of Adam and Eve* (which dates to the first century BC) as well as the fourth-century AD Christian Syriac text *The Book of the Cave of Treasures*. See Gabriel Said Reynolds, *The Qur'ān and the Bible: Text and commentary* (New Haven, CT: Yale University Press, 2018), pp. 38–39. The Qur'an seems to know of these traditions via oral tradition: see Andrew G. Bannister, *An Oral-Formulaic Study of the Qur'an* (New York: Lexington Books, 2014), especially pp. 29–30, 271–281.

has gone wrong with the world? In a word, no, for we must not simply observe that the Qur'an retells the story; we also need to ask *how* it retells it and in particular how it adapts the Adam and Eve story to Islamic theology. We need to pay careful attention and observe the key changes made to the story by the Qur'an.

The first striking observation is one that we noted in chapter 4, namely that the relationship motif has vanished. No longer is God walking in the garden with Adam and Eve and no longer is the story about trust; rather, the central theme has become advice and from where one receives it. A recurring theme throughout the Qur'an is that human beings are weak, frail and in constant need of guidance: Adam and Eve's basic mistake was to seek guidance from the wrong source. A few verses on from this story in the Qur'an, a little mini-sermon is given, explaining how humanity is divided into two groups: those whom Allah has guided and those – like Adam and Eve – whom Satan has guided:

O ye Children of Adam! Let not Satan seduce you, in the same manner as He got your parents out of the Garden, stripping them of their raiment, to expose their shame: for he and his tribe watch you from a position where ye cannot see them: We made the evil ones friends (only) to those without faith.

When they do aught that is shameful, they say: 'We found our fathers doing so'; and 'Allah commanded us thus': Say: 'Nay, Allah never commands what is shameful: do ye say of Allah what ye know not?'

Say: 'My Lord hath commanded justice; and that ye set your whole selves (to Him) at every time and place of prayer, and call upon Him, making your devotion sincere as in His sight: such as He created you in the beginning, so shall ye return.'

Some He hath guided: Others have (by their choice) deserved the loss of their way; in that they took the evil ones, in preference

to Allah, for their friends and protectors, and think that they receive guidance.
(Q. 7:27–30)

It is also clear from the Qur'an's retelling of the Adam and Eve story that this was not the point at which the problem began, for we are informed that the first human couple were shameful *before* their fall from the garden (see verse 20 above: 'all their shame that was hidden from them (before)'). The Qur'an has thus significantly reworked this story so it is no longer about the original fall of humanity and the root of our troubles but instead describes a mere slip: Adam and Eve were weak and shameful, should have followed Allah's guidance, but mistakenly listened to the wrong person. As the Ugandan Muslim theologian (and former ambassador to Saudi Arabia) Badru Kateregga puts it:

> The Christian witness that the rebellion by our first parents has tragically distorted man, and that sinfulness pervades us individually and collectively, is very contrary to Islamic witness. Islam teaches that the first phase of life on earth did not begin in sin and rebellion against Allah. Although Adam disobeyed Allah, he repented and was forgiven and even given guidance for mankind. Man is not born a sinner and the doctrine of the sinfulness of man has no basis in Islam.[10]

While the Qur'an may not develop the idea of human sinfulness into a full-blown doctrine, nevertheless it is certainly a theme to which it frequently returns. Humanity is regularly chastised for its lack of obedience, with the formulaic command 'Obey Allah and obey the Messenger!' (or 'Don't *disobey* Allah and his messenger') occurring dozens of times; for example: 'But whoever disobeys God and His

---

10 Badru D. Kateregga and David Shenk, *Islam and Christianity: A Muslim and a Christian in dialogue* (Grand Rapids, MI: Eerdmans, 1981), p. 101.

messenger, and transgresses His limits – He will cause him to enter the Fire, there to remain. For him (there is) a humiliating punishment' (Q. 4:14). In order to help its readers avoid disobeying Allah, the Qur'an contains many lists of wrong actions, with a differentiation made between 'great sins' (such as murder, adultery and pride) and lesser sins.

But what is the root cause of this human tendency to disobey Allah? The Qur'an does not explore the question in the same way as the Bible, but it offers a few hints. For example, there is the fact that human beings are forgetful:

On no soul doth Allah place a burden greater than it can bear. It gets every good that it earns, and it suffers every ill that it earns. (Pray:) 'Our Lord! Condemn us not *if we forget* or fall into error; our Lord!'
(Q. 2:286)[11]

The Qur'an also regularly points out that Allah created human beings weak and frail (just like Adam and his wife), in need of constant guidance and correction: 'God wishes to lighten (your burdens) for you, (for) *the human was created weak*' (Q. 4:28).

Finally, the Qur'an also repeatedly returns to the theme that humans are ignorant and stubborn, prone to going wrong in all kinds of ways despite Allah having sent them signs and guidance: 'If God had (so) pleased, He would indeed have gathered them to the guidance. Do not be one of the ignorant' (Q. 6:35).

Noticeably absent throughout the Qur'an's discussion of human sinfulness is any connection to the idea of covenant faithfulness. Nowhere in the Qur'an does Allah enter into mutual covenant commitments with humanity, nor does Allah invite humanity to be faithful to the covenant as he has been faithful. (Indeed, 'faithful' is

---

11 All emphasis in quotations from the Qur'an is mine.

not a description the Qur'an ever chooses to apply to Allah.) Quite simply, we have a very different theology here from that of the Bible, as Mark Durie explains:

> The Qur'an assumes a very different understanding of the fundamental human problem to that offered in Genesis. In the Qur'an's understanding, human beings like Adam and his wife are easily led astray. They are warned to follow the right guidance of Allah and not to be deceived by false guides. The human ancestors, Adam and his wife, serve as an object lesson in what happens when humans fail to follow right guidance: they are stripped naked and humiliated. In contrast, in the Bible human beings, whose nature is inherently opposed to God's ways and inclined to evil, fall into ever-worsening transgressions until finally God himself intervenes, repeatedly, to rescue and restore creation.[12]

Different diagnoses – different doctors?

When we experience a medical problem, the first step towards a cure is obtaining the correct diagnosis. One of my favourite hobbies is hill walking, and a few months ago I was descending a path through some woods below Skiddaw, the fourth-highest mountain in the English Lake District. Carelessly not watching where I was putting my feet, I trod on a tree root, slipped, spun simultaneously on three axes like a demented dervish, and landed heavily on one knee. There was a sickening crunch, a white-hot flash of pain and – after a visit to the doctor the next day – the diagnosis of an extremely bad sprain. It took several weeks of physiotherapy before I could walk without wincing.

---

12 Mark Durie, *The Qur'an and Its Biblical Reflexes: Investigations into the genesis of a religion* (Lanham, MD: Lexington Books, 2018), p. 228.

The very same month that I bashed my knee, a friend was diagnosed with cancer. What had begun as a minor annoying pain, one
he was tempted to dismiss, refused to disappear. After a visit to his
doctor and a battery of tests, it turned out that he was facing a life-
threatening cancer, and many months of chemotherapy lay ahead
before he was finally cured.

Two different conditions; two very different diagnoses; two
entirely different treatment regimes. And just as when it comes to
our health we want to know whether we are facing a sprain or a
tumour, similarly when it comes to the question of what has gone
wrong with the world and especially our part in that wrongness, we
want the proper diagnosis. Both the Bible and the Qur'an talk about
human sinfulness, but is that problem more like a sore knee (so we
need exercise and encouragement), or is it more like cancer (so
we need real help and intervention)?

What has gone wrong with the world? The Bible's diagnosis is that
our rebellion and unfaithfulness have led to separation from God
and the corruption and twisting of our very nature. And while God's
laws and commandments can *highlight* our predicament, they cannot
solve the problem.

By contrast, the Qur'an's diagnosis is not nearly so serious. Human
beings were created weak, fallible and forgetful – and those frailties
led to us being removed from paradise. All we need is to follow the
right instructions, the right guidance, and we can find our way back.

But what does all of this say about God? Do these two quite
different diagnoses shed any light on the question of whether Allah
and Yahweh are in any sense the same? Absolutely they do, for these
two very different understandings of what has gone wrong with the
world flow out of the nature and character of God.

As we saw in chapter 4, Yahweh is a god who is relational,
knowable and loving – a god who binds himself in covenant commitment to humanity, a god who created us for relationship and
who invites us to call him 'Father'. But Yahweh is also a god who is

holy, utterly morally pure, and unable even to tolerate sin in his presence. Our sinfulness has caused humanity to be unfit for the presence of a god like this – and thus we are alienated from god and, as the ribbon of cracks has spread, alienated from proper relationships with one another and the world.

When it comes to Allah, however, the Qur'an does not describe him in the way that the Bible describes Yahweh. Allah is never called 'Father' but is solely a lord and master, giving guidance and help at times, yes, but not offering relationship or covenant faithfulness. Out of those two very different views of god's nature flow two very different understandings of what it means to be human – and two very different diagnoses of what has gone wrong with the world.

So which diagnosis is correct? Which diagnosis best fits reality, which most accurately describes the state of our world – not merely the depths of evil to which humanity has sunk, the damage we have wrought to one another and creation, but also our everyday proclivities to nastiness? Does it look, realistically and honestly, as if we are dealing with something more like a bad knee or something more like a cancer? I want to suggest that the Bible's far more serious diagnosis maps far better on to the reality of our lived experience. As the philosopher and novelist G. K. Chesterton is reputed to have remarked, commenting on the Christian claim that human nature has become corrupt: this is the only religious doctrine that has been empirically validated by two thousand years of bloody and tragic human history.[13]

The two very different visions of god and his identity offered by the Bible and the Qur'an have, as we have already seen, some major implications. They affect not merely what we think about god, about humanity and about what's gone wrong with our world; they also directly affect the question of what might be the cure for our broken world. It is to that most important of questions that we now turn.

---

13 Cited in Alan Jacobs, *Original Sin: A cultural history* (London: SPCK, 2008), p. x.

Key takeaways

- Most people are wise enough to realize that the world is broken in all kinds of ways (and that we are not just innocent victims but are guilty of our part in that brokenness). The question is *why* is the world broken? That's a question that every religion, philosophy or political system tries to answer.

- For the Bible, the basic problem is that human beings are deeply affected by sin, our very nature corrupted and twisted. This has separated us from the close relationship with God for which we were designed, as well as alienated us from one another and from the rest of creation.

- For the Qur'an, human beings were not created for relationship with God but intended simply to obey. However, humans are weak and fallible, flawed and forgetful, and frequently end up disobeying Allah's commands.

- Islam and Christianity thus have very different answers to the question 'What has gone wrong with the world?' – answers that flow naturally from their very different understanding of who god is and who and what he designed humans to be.

7

Self-help or salvation?
The Qur'an, the Bible and the cure
for all that ails us

During my twenties, I suffered from a terrible phobia about flying. It's not that I wouldn't get on a plane, but in the days leading up to a flight I would increasingly panic. In the hours spent at the airport before departure, I would contemplate heading to the lavatory and escaping from the terminal[1] through a window; and on the flight itself, I would sit bolt upright, arms rigid and knuckles white, wondering when the wings would fall off or the engines explode. Sometimes I would pass the time calculating how long it would take us to fall to the ground should gravity cast a glance our way, notice many tons of aluminium in the wrong place and cause us to plummet earthwards like a concrete donkey.

I probably made my condition worse by my addiction to air-crash documentaries. My wife would often discover me slumped on the sofa, watching some flaming wreck on the TV and muttering, 'If God had intended us to fly, he would never have invented the railways.' My favourite air-crash show was the Canadian series *Mayday*, and one episode, 'Fatal Distraction', sticks in my mind. It tells the story of Eastern Airlines Flight 401, which crashed into a Florida swamp, killing 101 passengers and crew. Unusually, the cause was not mechanical failure but very human error – the flight crew got distracted by a faulty landing-gear indicator light and as they tried to solve that issue (even taking the light assembly to pieces), they

---

1   Whoever first thought of calling the building from which flights depart the 'terminal' clearly hadn't thought this one through.

failed to address the far more serious problem, namely that the auto-pilot had become disconnected and the plane was slowly descending into the ground. By the time they noticed, it was too late to save their stricken aircraft.

I eventually conquered my fear of flying with the help of a friendly pilot who spent hours answering my inane questions ('No, the wings won't fall off'; 'Neither will the vertical stabilizer'; 'No, you can't accidentally open the emergency exit while looking for the lavatory'; 'Have you considered taking the train next time?'). But I retained my love of the *Mayday* documentary, not least because, as the case of Flight 401 demonstrates, its episodes are often poignant reminders of the importance of both diagnosing the right problem and applying the right solution. While it is certainly illuminating to have every warning light in the cockpit working, it is arguably more important not to fly into the ground. The right solution really matters.

The TV documentary took its title, *Mayday*, from the word commonly used as a call sign by aviators and mariners to declare a life-threatening emergency. The term 'mayday' was first coined by Frederick Mockford, a radio operator at Croydon Airport in London, who had been asked to come up with a word that could be used to signify an emergency. Given that most air traffic at the time was between London and Paris, Mockford chose 'mayday', from the French *m'aidez*, which means 'help me'.[2]

Given all the brokenness in the world, this cry for help is highly appropriate to our fourth world-view question: 'What's the solution?' We clearly need help, but what kind of help? And in particular, do we just need *self-help* (a motivational pep talk, an encouragement to stand up straight with our shoulders back and get on with it) or

---

2 Other famous distress signals or codewords include the Morse code letters 'SOS' (short for 'save our souls'), 'Pan-Pan' (from the French for 'help, I have no bread') and, in the Bannister house, 'Spider! Spider! Spider!', a sign that one of the smaller members of the family has discovered an eight-legged invader, usually the size of a fingernail, that clearly is threatening to eat us all.

do we actually need *saving*? Can we simply help ourselves or do we need help from outside?

In the previous three chapters, we have seen tremendous differences opening up between Allah, the God of the Qur'an, and Yahweh, the God of the Bible, as we have explored the first three world-view questions. As we have looked at god's identity, at what it means to be human and at what has gone wrong with the world, we have seen that Allah and Yahweh are described entirely differently, have created human beings in very different ways and for very different purposes, and have quite different things to say about what has gone wrong with things. Let's now dig into the Qur'an and the Bible to explore what Allah and Yahweh have to say about the solution to the problems affecting us and the world.

What *type* of help does the Qur'an think we need?

One of the threads that has run throughout this book is the warning that when it comes to thinking about different religions, it is all too easy to assume that every religion has the same basic understanding of reality. This can happen when we take the religion we know best (often for Westerners this is Christianity, even if it is a half-remembered, slightly anaemic version we caught bits of at school), and then we look at other religions through this lens. And so we ask questions like 'What does Islam say we have to do to find salvation?' or 'Is Islam or Christianity better able to save us?' But what if salvation and being saved are not particularly Islamic concepts? What if asking a question like 'How are we saved in Islam?' is tantamount to asking how one scores runs in tennis or rugby?[3] This

---

3 I owe this analogy to Stephen Prothero, *God Is Not One: The eight rival religions that run the world* (New York: HarperOne, 2010), p. 22.

is, of course, a category error: 'runs' is a cricketing term and is a foreign idea to other sports, such as tennis or rugby.[4]

Similarly, I want to suggest that 'salvation' and 'being saved' are foreign ideas to the Qur'an and to Islam. When one looks at the Qur'an, it is striking how rarely the noun 'salvation' or the verb 'to be saved' is used. In the first case, the Arabic word *furqān*, often translated by English editions of the Qur'an as 'salvation' or 'deliverance' in the seven places it occurs, seems in most cases to refer not to Allah's act of rescuing humanity but to some kind of book. For example: 'And [remember] when We gave to Moses the Book and the Salvation [*al-furqān*], that haply you should be guided' (Q. 2:53).

Meanwhile, verbs derived from the Arabic root *njw* (meaning 'save', 'deliver', 'rescue', 'escape') occur about eighty times[5] in the Qur'an and are almost exclusively used to describe Allah's act of rescuing a particular person, usually one of his messengers. For example, it occurs when the Qur'an summarizes the story of Noah and how God rescued him and his family from the waters of the flood: 'Certainly Noah called on Us, and excellent indeed were the responders! We *rescued* him and his family from great distress' (Q. 37:75–76).

For the Qur'an, Allah can certainly act to rescue particular individuals or groups of people, but there is no overarching plan of salvation. Nowhere is Allah ever called 'saviour' or 'deliverer'; nor, indeed, is there any Arabic word used in the Qur'an that means either of those things. As the Islamic scholar Ismail al-Faruqi wrote:

[I]n the Islamic view, human beings are no more 'fallen' than they are 'saved'. Because they are not 'fallen', they have no need

---

4 'Runs' is often a foreign term, it must be said, to certain national cricket teams.

5 Word-count statistics such as this one have been produced using Qur'an Gateway (<www.qurangateway.org>), an innovative software tool for easily searching and analysing the Qur'an.

of a saviour. But because they are not 'saved' either, they need to do good works – and do them ethically – which alone will earn them the desired 'salvation'. Indeed, salvation is an improper term, since to need 'salvation', one must be in a predicament beyond the hope of ever escaping it. But [according to Islam] men and women are not in that predicament.[6]

In other words, what Allah seems to be offering is a self-help programme. Here is guidance and moral instruction – follow the guidance, keep the commands, guard yourself from evil, do good works, and thus, by your own effort and hard work, you can help yourself and become successful, earning forgiveness and avoiding the punishment of hellfire:

Fear the Fire, which is repaired for those who reject Faith: And *obey* Allah and the Messenger; that ye may obtain mercy.

Be quick in the race for forgiveness from your Lord, and for a Garden whose width is that (of the whole) of the heavens and of the earth, prepared for the righteous –

Those who spend (freely), whether in prosperity, or in adversity; who restrain anger, and pardon (all) men – for Allah loves those who do good – And those who, having done something to be ashamed of, or wronged their own souls, earnestly bring Allah to mind, and ask for forgiveness for their sins – and who can forgive sins except Allah? – and are never obstinate in persisting knowingly in (the wrong) they have done.

For such the *reward* is forgiveness from their Lord, and Gardens with rivers flowing underneath – an eternal dwelling: How excellent a recompense for those who work (and strive)! (Q. 3:131–136)

---

6   Ismail al-Faruqi, *Islam* (Niles, IL: Argus, 1984 [1979]), p. 9.

One question raised by that qur'anic passage concerns whether forgiveness that is paid as a reward is actually forgiveness. For example, suppose that one morning at breakfast, tired from a bad night's sleep and irritable from discovering we have run out of coffee, I say something short-tempered and rude to my wife, Astrid. Later that day, feeling guilty about how I treated her, I say, 'Honey, I'm very sorry for how I spoke to you this morning; will you please forgive me?' Astrid looks thoughtful for a moment and then replies, 'Absolutely, of course I'll forgive you. You just need to take out the rubbish each week for the rest of the year and also buy me a shrubbery (a nice one and not too expensive).' So has she forgiven me? No, clearly not; what we have here is not forgiveness but economics. Astrid has not forgiven me; she has just named her price. And if I complete my tasks successfully, I have not been forgiven. Rather, I have *earned* my way back into favour (and in the process, she will have become indebted to me – she will have a duty to forgive me as I have paid the price in full). This is light years away from forgiveness, which by its very nature must be free for the one receiving it.

What *type* of help does the Bible think we need?

When we turn to the Bible and ask the question 'What kind of help do we need?', we see a very different answer. This should not surprise us, for as we saw in chapter 6, the Qur'an and the Bible differ greatly over the question of what has gone wrong with us: are we simply a little forgetful, bumbling our way through life like Homer Simpson on a bad day, or is there something more deeply wrong with us? The Bible thinks there is, that it isn't simply a case of us not knowing what to do. We know what we *should* do; we just don't seem to be able to do it. So sending us additional commands and moral instructions potentially makes things worse, exposing our inadequacy even more. Just as when I say to my five-year-old son, 'Please don't touch that chocolate cake', and his eyes light up greedily (he hadn't even *thought* about cake, but now it's a real possibility, no matter what Dad says), so, the Bible teaches, this is what happens to us when God reveals his law:

> I would not have known what sin was had it had not been for the law. For I would not have known what coveting really was if the law had not said, 'You shall not covet.' But sin, seizing the opportunity afforded by the commandment, produced in me every kind of coveting. For apart from the law, sin was dead . . . I found that the very commandment that was intended to bring life actually brought death. For sin, seizing the opportunity afforded by the commandment, deceived me, and through the commandment put me to death.
> (Romans 7:7–8, 10–11)

Time and again the Bible teaches that at the very heart of our being we are rebels: drastically and determinedly in rebellion against God and all that he has asked of us. As John Stott, one of the most influential Christian theologians of the twentieth century, put it:

> We have rejected the position of dependence that our created-ness inevitably involves and made a bid for independence. Worse still, we have dared to proclaim our self-dependence, our autonomy, which is to claim the position occupied by God alone. Sin is not a regrettable lapse from conventional standards; its essence is hostility to God.[7]

Because Yahweh is a God who is holy – utterly morally pure, the very definition of goodness and justice – we have a real problem as human beings, in that our brokenness and rebellion mean we are

---

7 John Stott, *The Cross of Christ* (Downers Grove, IL: IVP, 2006 [1986]), p. 82.

radically separated from God. This means we need more than just self-help – we are in need of saving. We actually need salvation. That's the *bad* news. The *good* news is that salvation is a key biblical idea, the word occurring hundreds of times throughout the Bible.

In the Old Testament, 'saviour' is a word frequently applied to Yahweh as a name or title; for example: 'Yahweh lives! Blessed be my rock! Exalted be God my *saviour*' (Psalm 18:46, author's translation). Salvation is frequently offered as a hope and a promise for those who reach out to Yahweh and ask for his help: 'Everyone who calls on the name of Yahweh will be *saved*' (Joel 2:32, author's translation).

In the New Testament, salvation continues to be a major theme, centring particularly on Jesus' death on the cross, the means through which salvation is offered to the whole world:

> For God so loved the world that he gave his one and only Son, that whoever believes in him shall not perish but have eternal life. For God did not send his Son into the world to condemn the world, but to *save* the world through him.
> (John 3:16–17)

For the Bible, we need more than just assistance, more than guidance; rather, we need salvation. We need more than a moral exemplar, a teacher or a guru; rather, we need a saviour and a rescuer. After all, there is little point in fixing a malfunctioning light bulb if the plane is minutes away from crashing into the muddy waters of a Florida swamp.

More than mere guidance

Self-help or salvation? That question gets to the heart of whether or not we are speaking of the same god when we talk about Allah and Yahweh. The nature of the problem diagnosed and the type of help offered expose real and significant differences. Let me illustrate further by way of an analogy.

I am an avid mountain climber and love scrambling across ridges, summits and high places. But some years back, I upped the ante slightly and decided to try rock climbing. The sport and I never fully hit it off, not least because there was something existentially troubling about trusting one's life to a soggy rope and a few bits of metal jammed hopefully into crevices. But suppose I had become really keen and decided, after a few months of practice, to make my way to California's Yosemite Valley in order to attempt to climb – solo – the face of El Capitan, a 3,000-foot sheer granite monolith that is one of the world's hardest rock climbs. Unsurprisingly, I get completely stuck, about 200 feet up, and am now cragfast, perched on a narrow ledge above a vertiginous drop. In terror, I begin crying out 'Help! Help!' at the top of my voice.

Before long, a pair of climbers appear at the bottom of the rock face and I immediately recognize one of them – it's the world-famous rock climber Alex Honnold, who has ascended El Capitan many times. Indeed, he has even climbed it both solo and unroped, a remarkable feat documented in the 2018 film *Free Solo*. Alex begins shouting up encouragement: 'It's easy! Move your thumb an inch to the left; move your left foot down a fraction! You can *do* it! What doesn't kill you makes you stronger!' The unknown climber, on the other hand, begins roping up and shouts up, 'Stay exactly where you are! I'll come and get you!'

It matters not that Alex is arguably the world's greatest climber who has ascended El Capitan so many times that he knows every inch of the rock. That makes not one iota of a difference; for, in my desperate predicament, I don't need expert advice, guidance, or quotes from motivational posters. What I *need* is rescuing and saving. Thus, I will take an anonymous climber with the offer of salvation over the world's greatest rock climber bearing mere advice any time.

Sometimes instruction, advice and guidance – even if they come from a world-renowned expert – are simply not enough. Sometimes we actually need rescuing, and that rescue may prove costly to the rescuer (my anonymous rock-climbing saviour put his own life at risk to rescue me). And just as for our physical safety, so for our spiritual safety. With Allah and the Qur'an, all that is on offer is guidance; for Yahweh and the Bible, what is on offer is rescue – and a rescue that, as we shall see later, comes at great cost to the rescuer.

The Qur'an's *method* of help

So the Qur'an and the Bible offer very different types of help. But what do their different solutions look like in practice? What is the *method* you might use to access these respective types of help? After all, it is one thing to *have* help; it is another thing to *apply* that help correctly. This is why medicines, for example, often have accompanying leaflets helpfully explaining their correct use.[8]

The Qur'an's approach to this question begins by noting that humans are forgetful and neglectful of Allah's commands and guidance: 'Do not be like those who forgot God, and He caused them to forget their own selves. Those – they are the wicked' (Q. 59:19).

In response, Allah has sent down commands and instructions with his messengers:

The messenger believes in what has been sent down to him from his Lord, and (so do) the believers. Each one believes in God, and His angels, and His Books, and His messengers. We make no distinction between any of His messengers. And they

---

8 The packet of plasters that I used recently after my son cut his head (while experimenting to see whether it is possible to jump on Lego bricks and surf across the floor) bore this helpful warning: 'For external use only'. There are clearly some *very* confused people out there.

say, 'We hear and obey. (Grant us) Your forgiveness, our Lord.
To You is the (final) destination.'
(Q. 2:285)

If human beings keep these commands, obeying Allah and his
messenger, then that obedience will earn them forgiveness: '[Allah]
may reward those who believe and work deeds of righteousness: for
such is Forgiveness and a Sustenance Most Generous' (Q. 34:4).

The Qur'an is very clear that nobody else can help you with your
burden of sin. Rather, you must carry it wholly yourself: 'Whoever
is (rightly) guided, is guided only for himself, and whoever goes
astray, goes astray only against himself. No one bearing a burden
bears the burden of another' (Q. 17:15).

If you work hard at moral improvement, then you have a chance
to become one of the successful ones,[9] avoiding hellfire and earning
the reward of paradise: 'Those are limits set by Allah: those who obey
Allah and His Messenger will be admitted to Gardens with rivers
flowing beneath, to abide therein (for ever) and that will be the
supreme achievement' (Q. 4:13).

The qur'anic method of self-help, of consistent effort and striving
to ensure that your actions set you up for success in the afterlife, is
summarized well by the British-Pakistani Muslim writer Ziauddin
Sardar. In his book *Desperately Seeking Paradise*, which tells the story
of his struggles as a young Muslim to make sense of these questions,
Sardar writes:

Paradise and hell, the two sides of the same coin: that is the
Islamic notion of the hereafter . . . In between, the fulcrum on
the plane of time between the here and now and the Hereafter,

---

9 'Success' is a major qur'anic concept; for example, the phrase 'mighty triumph/success'
(*al-fawzu l-'aẓīmu*) occurs sixteen times (see Q. 4:13, 73; 5:119; 9:72, 89, 100, 111; 10:64;
33:71; 37:60; 40:9; 44:57; 48:5; 57:12; 61:12; 64:9). Arguably, the Qur'an is far more
concerned with how to be successful than how to be saved.

is the Day of Judgement, where each will be held responsible for their actions in life. The actions of our earthly existence must stand the test of that day. They must be measured against the ideal life of prayer, devotion to humility, equality, pursuit of knowledge and justice.[10]

The Qur'an's method of help is incredibly simple: work hard, do the right thing, earn your reward. But what if the problem with our world is not that we do not know the right thing to do, but rather that we lack the power actually to do it? What if our problem is not ignorance or forgetfulness of God's law, but our inability to keep it? If our basic problem is that our natural instinct on seeing a law is to break it, on seeing a moral edict to ignore it, if we struggle to be good and do the right thing, then Allah's method of sending down additional commands is of little use. It's a bit like seeing a man drowning in a lake and helpfully offering to toss him a bucket of water. He doesn't need more of what is already killing him; what he needs is rescue.

The Bible's *method* of help

The Bible's method of help looks very different from all of this. Its approach begins, as we saw in chapter 6, with the recognition that human beings are separated by our sinfulness and rebellion from a God who is both a loving Father and also utterly holy and righteous:

Your iniquities have separated
    you from your God;
your sins have hidden his face from you,
    so that he will not hear.
(Isaiah 59:2)

10 Ziauddin Sardar, *Desperately Seeking Paradise: Journeys of a sceptical Muslim* (London: Granta, 2005), p. 336.

Despite our rebellion, Yahweh desires reconciliation and covenant relationship with us, so he created a way whereby our wrongdoing – which rightly deserved death – could be forgiven by another dying in our place. In the Old Testament, this happened through the sacrificial system that God instituted – rituals in which an animal could symbolically atone for the sins of a worshipper by dying in his or her place:[11] 'For the life of a creature is in the blood, and I have given it to you to make atonement for yourselves on the altar; it is the blood that makes atonement for one's life' (Leviticus 17:11). But the blood of animals could never ultimately and finally deal with human sinfulness and the brokenness of the world. Rather, the sacrificial system was a sign that pointed forward to something much greater, the once-for-all perfect sacrifice of Jesus:

> The law is only a shadow of the good things that are coming – not the realities themselves. For this reason it can never, by the same sacrifices repeated endlessly year after year, make perfect those who draw near to worship ... It is impossible for the blood of bulls and goats to take away sins ...
>
> [Jesus] said, 'Sacrifices and offerings, burnt offerings and sin offerings you did not desire, nor were you pleased with them' – though they were offered in accordance with the law. Then he said, 'Here I am, I have come to do your will.' He sets aside the first to establish the second. And by that will, we have been made holy through the sacrifice of the body of Jesus Christ once for all.
>
> (Hebrews 10:1, 4, 8–10)

At the climax of his earthly ministry, Jesus took a central symbol of Judaism – the Passover meal that faithful Jews would eat each year to commemorate God's rescue of them from Egypt in the exodus

---

11 See the helpful discussion of the Old Testament sacrifice system in Stott, *Cross*, pp. 134–135.

over a thousand years before – and reshaped it around himself and his intention to offer his life as a sacrifice of redemption, the basis for a whole new covenant relationship between God and humanity:

> While they were eating, Jesus took bread, and when he had given thanks, he broke it and gave it to his disciples, saying, 'Take it; this is my body.'
>
> Then he took a cup, and when he had given thanks, he gave it to them, and they all drank from it.
>
> 'This is my blood of the covenant, which is poured out for many,' he said to them.
>
> (Mark 14:22–24)

At the heart of the Bible's method for dealing with human broken-ness and the shambles our world is in lies the death of Jesus, making atonement once and for all for our sinfulness: 'God presented Christ as a sacrifice of atonement, through the shedding of his blood – to be received by faith. He did this to demonstrate his righteousness, because in his forbearance he had left the sins committed beforehand unpunished' (Romans 3:25).

The Bible is clear: our situation and condition are drastic; our nature is corrupt and our lives and actions render us unable to be in the presence of a holy God. But Yahweh in his faithfulness has made a way back, has offered a rescue plan that means we can be truly forgiven. Jesus' close disciple, Peter, explained this to an audience in Jerusalem after he had preached the very first Christian sermon in history and people had asked him how to be saved. Peter replied, 'Repent and be baptised, every one of you, in the name of Jesus Christ for the forgiveness of your sins. And you will receive the gift of the Holy Spirit' (Acts 2:38).

However, the solution that the Bible sets out does not just concern forgiveness and the restoration of our relationship with God; it also offers the promise of an entirely new nature to replace our old sinful one:[12] 'So if anyone is in Christ, there is a new creation: everything old has passed away; see, everything has become new!' (2 Corinthians 5:17 NRSV). He or she will also, the Bible promises, be filled with God's Spirit and given the power to live differently; rather than good deeds being the *means* of salvation (as in the Qur'an), they become the *result* of salvation: 'The fruit of the Spirit is love, joy, peace, forbearance, kindness, goodness, faithfulness, gentleness and self-control' (Galatians 5:22–23).

Good advice versus good news

We have seen that Allah and Yahweh offer very different solutions to the brokenness in our world. In short, for the Qur'an the *problem* is human ignorance and forgetfulness; the *solution* is knowledge and information. By contrast, for the Bible, the *problem* is our sinful nature and alienation from God; the *solution* is atonement and transformation.

These two very different approaches can be neatly illustrated by comparing the first sura of the Qur'an, *al-Fātiḥah* ('The Opening'), with the Lord's Prayer that Jesus taught to his disciples. Faithful Muslims recite sura *al-Fātiḥah* many times daily, for its text is an integral part of the Islamic ritual prayers. At its heart lies this request: '*Guide* us to the straight path' (Q. 1:6).

By comparison, consider the Lord's Prayer, which for two thousand years has been an integral part of Christian devotional life, both individually and corporately, with many churches including it as part of their liturgies. At its centre lies this plea: '*Forgive* us our sins' (Luke 11:4).

The key idea for Islam is *guidance*. The key idea for Christianity is *forgiveness*.[13] This difference is crucial, because guidance (no

---

12 See also John 3:3–7 where Jesus uses the metaphor of being 'born again' to describe the experience of inward transformation offered to those who follow him.

13 I owe this point to Mark Durie: see *The Qur'an and Its Biblical Reflexes*, p. 227; see also Gordon D. Nickel, *The Quran with Christian Commentary: A guide to understanding the scripture of Islam* (Grand Rapids, MI: Zondervan Academic, 2020), p. 34.

matter how precise) and moral commands (no matter how detailed) cannot address the basic issue of sinfulness and the human heart. To truly deal with that, the Bible says that what we actually need is forgiveness and salvation, which means that we need a saviour, and that is why Jesus came and gave his life on the cross. For the Bible, Jesus is not just a moral guide or an example to follow, but a rescuer and a saviour.

For Muslim readers of the Bible, the atoning sacrifice of Jesus for human sin is a difficulty, largely because of the Qur'an's insistence that 'no bearer of burdens can bear the burdens of another'.[14] But notice that despite its very different theology, even the Qur'an does not actually say that *nobody* can carry the burden of sin of another. Rather, it says that someone who is burdened by his or her own sin has no spare capacity to help another. Yet one of the points on which the Bible *and* the Qur'an agree is that Jesus was sinless.[15] Thus I sometimes ask Muslim friends, 'Could it be possible that one who had no burden of sin of his own to carry might be able to carry ours?'

Desperately seeking paradise

So far, we have seen that both the type and the method of help applied to solving the brokenness, injustice and suffering in us and the world are radically different in the Qur'an and the Bible. But what about the final destination of humans? If one follows the Qur'an's self-help programme or responds to the Bible's offer of rescue and salvation, where might one arrive?

---

14 Q. 6:164; 17:15; 35:18; 39:7; 53:38.

15 On the sinlessness of Jesus in the Bible, see for example John 17:5; 2 Corinthians 5:21; Hebrews 4:15; 1 Peter 3:22; 1 John 3:5. On the sinlessness of Jesus in the Qur'an, see Q. 19:19. The hadith later developed this idea, with a tradition explaining that both Jesus and his mother, Mary, were sinless because Allah had protected them from Satan: 'Abu Huraira reported Allah's Messenger [Muhammad] as saying: No child is born but he is pricked by the satan and he begins to weep because of the pricking of the satan *except the son of Mary and his mother*' (Sahih Muslim 2366, my emphasis; see also Sahih al-Bukhari 3286; 4548).

Most people assume the answer to that question is 'heaven'. As someone who often speaks on interfaith issues, I know that one of the most common questions to come from audiences is 'Don't all religions lead to paradise?'[16] It turns out that, like cricket, things are considerably more complicated than that.

Beginning with the Qur'an, it mentions paradise just twice (Q. 18:107; 23:11).[17] Instead, the Qur'an's preferred word for what we would think of as 'heaven' is *jannah*, meaning 'garden',[18] an image that occurs over seventy times in the Qur'an:

A parable of the Garden which is promised to the ones who guard (themselves): In it (there are) rivers of water without pollution, and rivers of milk – its taste does not change – and rivers of wine – delicious to the drinkers – and rivers of purified honey. In it (there is) every (kind of) fruit for them, and forgiveness from their Lord. (Are they) like those who remain in the Fire? They are given boiling water to drink, and it cuts their insides (to pieces).
(Q. 47:15)

Elsewhere, the Qur'an speaks of the heavenly women, or 'houris', who will be given to male believers for sexual pleasure: 'Surely for the ones who guard (themselves) (there is) a (place of) safety: orchards and grapes, and full-breasted (maidens), (all) of the same age, and a cup full (of wine)' (Q. 78:31–34).[19]

---

16 The second most common question is 'Where *did* you get that joke from?'

17 When it mentions paradise, the Qur'an uses the word *firdaws*, a loanword that has come into Arabic from Greek. The Greek word is *parádeisos*, itself a loanword from the Persian word *pairidaēza*, which seems to have meant a circular enclosure, probably a garden or park. See Arthur Jeffery, *The Foreign Vocabulary of the Qur'an* (Leiden: Brill, 2007 [1938]), pp. 223–224.

18 As a keen but startlingly amateur gardener, I'm sure there are many words you might use for my garden, but 'paradise' and 'heaven' would not be among them; 'war zone' might be a more appropriate choice, especially after my children have been in it for more than five minutes.

19 See also Q. 44:54; 52:20; 55:72; 56:22.

Later Islamic theology is full of speculation about what the women of paradise will be like, with some traditions explaining how Allah will renew their virginity every time they have sex with their designated believer.[20] On the popular Islam Question & Answer website, run by Saudi Muslim scholar Shaykh al-Munajjid, a questioner asks about sexual intercourse with houris, and in the *fatwa* (ruling on Islamic law) given in response, the Muslim cleric explains how Muslim men will be given special strength to enjoy this aspect of paradise:

A man will be given the strength of a hundred men to eat, drink, feel desire, and have sexual intercourse. It was narrated from Anas (may Allah be pleased with him) that the Prophet (peace and blessings of Allah be upon him) said: 'The believer in Paradise will be given such and such strength for sexual intercourse.' He was asked, 'O Messenger of Allah, will he really be able to do that?' He said, 'He will be given the strength of one hundred (men).'[21]

Wine and women, fruit and water:[22] these are the very best that the qur'anic paradise has to offer. Yet what is most noticeable about this view of heaven is not what it contains but what – or rather *who* – is missing. God seems conspicuous by his absence. The Qur'an does not entice its readers with a vision of one day meeting Allah;[23] rather, eternity consists of wine, women and feasting.

20 See Gabriel Said Reynolds, *Allah: God in the Qur'an* (New Haven, CT: Yale University Press, 2020), p. 87, which notes how many Islamic exegetes connected this idea with Q. 56:36–37, which says: 'Surely We [Allah] produced them specially and made them virgins.'

21 'Will men in paradise have intercourse with *al-hoor aliyn*?', Question 10053, Islam Question & Answer, 30 August 2000, <https://islamqa.info/en/answers/10053/will-men-in-paradise-have-intercourse-with-al-hoor-aliyn>.The tradition cited from Anas in the *fatwa* comes from the hadith collection of al-Tirmidhi, no. 2459.

22 Which does, I admit, sound rather like the title of a vegan-friendly country-and-western album.

23 Some have suggested that in the Qur'an there are at least hints of the idea that one might meet Allah; for example, Q. 75:23 says that the blessed will 'gaze upon their Lord'. However, reading that verse in context, it becomes apparent that this passage is talking about the day of judgment, not describing the experience of the righteous in paradise.

But there is a problem: even if individuals do reach paradise, can they be sure they will remain there? Given that the Qur'an implies that paradise represents a return to the place from where Adam and his wife were evicted, a troubling conundrum arises: Adam sinned *in paradise* and was evicted. So how can we be sure the same will not happen to us?

Suppose somebody follows the Qur'an's programme of moral self-improvement and performs enough good works that he or she makes it to paradise – and it's wonderful: the wine, the food, the houris. But then one terrible day the righteous believer chokes on a date, trips over the cat,[24] blasphemes profusely and as a result is cast out. In short: how can a Muslim be sure that he or she will remain in paradise *even after making it there*? Unlike in Christianity, with its teaching that followers of Jesus are sanctified and transformed (upgraded to Human 2.0, as it were) before they enter life after death, Islam offers no personal transformation. There is no upgrade, just Human 1.0 – weak, fallible and morally flawed. The qur'anic Adam and his wife sinned in heaven and were evicted, a fate that could presumably happen to anybody.

But there is another, equally troubling problem with the Qur'an's view of paradise. In his classic book, *Islam: A comprehensive introduction*, world-renowned Pakistani Muslim theologian Javed Ahmad Ghamidi makes this remark about heaven: '[T]he Qur'ān has said that the dwellers of Paradise will get *whatever they desire*' (Q. 41:31; 43:71; 50:35).[25]

A few years back, I took part in a public dialogue at McGill University in Canada with a local Muslim imam, a younger scholar popular with Muslim students on campus. During the question-and-answer session, an audience member asked us both what we

---

24 I can already hear some readers protesting, 'Cats? In heaven? But aren't they . . . *evil*?' To which I say that you cannot judge the entirety of the cat race by Mr Bigglesworth.

25 Javed Ahmad Ghamidi, *Islam: A comprehensive introduction* (Lahore: Al-Mawrid, 2009), p. 189, my emphasis.

thought heaven was like. The imam went first and explained how he loved playing basketball. 'So for me,' he said, 'heaven will be like the most amazing basketball court – and wherever I throw the ball from, no matter how difficult the shot, I will always shoot and score!'[26]

His face glowed as he described what, for him, was clearly a beautiful vision, and so I felt awkward asking the obvious question: 'What happens if you get bored?'

'What do you mean?' he asked, looking worried.

'When you've spent an hour or two throwing balls from all over the court and discovering there is no challenge – you literally cannot miss – won't boredom set in? And what about after a day, or a week, a month, or a year? And that's just the beginning of *eternity*.'

His face fell and I was reminded of the words originally attributed to G. K. Chesterton: 'Meaninglessness does not come from being weary of pain; meaninglessness comes from being weary of pleasure.'[27]

What happens if you get the pleasure you desire, but that pleasure offers rapidly diminishing returns? This idea is powerfully explored in a 1960 episode of the American TV show *The Twilight Zone*. Called 'A Nice Place to Visit', the episode tells the story of a petty criminal, Henry 'Rocky' Valentine, who is killed and wakes up in a beautiful apartment complex. He is given all the money, wine and women he wants and at first it seems wonderful. But after a month of this, Rocky has become bored. He tells the spiritual being, named Pip, assigned to look after him that he's tired of heaven and that he'd much prefer to go 'to the other place'. At which Pip replies with an evil laugh, '*Heaven?* Whatever gave you the idea you were in heaven, Mr Valentine? This *is* the other place!' As the credits roll, the narrator

---

26 As somebody who is considerably shorter than 6 ft, basketball at school was a traumatic experience. In later life, I discovered the joys of croquet: at least if I miss a shot, I can amuse myself by running under the hoops.

27 G. K. Chesterton, 'The Everlasting Man' (1925), paraphrased here in Ravi Zacharias, *Can Man Live without God?* (Nashville, TN: W Publishing, 1994), pp. 178–179.

says, 'Now he has everything he's ever wanted – and he's going to have to live with it for eternity.'[28]

This is exactly the problem with the Qur'an's vision of paradise: it is not deep enough to sustain someone for *months*, let alone *eternity*. You see, I love food;[29] I enjoy a bottle of wine every now and then; I think that sex is one of God's great inventions and I have been happily married for twenty-two years.[30] But however fine the food, wonderful the wine or sublime the sex, how long before the pleasure fades? Eventually you begin asking, like Henry Valentine, 'Is there more than this?', and the answer is: no, welcome to eternity. Viewed this way, the Qur'an's vision of eternity looks less like heaven and more like a living nightmare.

Not presents but *presence*

The Bible offers a remarkably different vision of eternal life. Rather than a heavenly party, the Bible describes how Yahweh will not just recreate our physical bodies but will also renew heaven and earth, where he will then dwell with his people for eternity:[31]

> Then I saw 'a new heaven and a new earth,' for the first heaven and the first earth had passed away, and there was no longer any sea. I saw the Holy City, the new Jerusalem, coming down out of heaven from God, prepared as a bride beautifully dressed for her husband. And I heard a loud voice from the throne saying, 'Look! God's dwelling-place is now among the people, and he will dwell with them. They will be his people, and God himself will be with them and be their God. 'He will wipe every tear

---

28 For a modern take on a similar idea, check out the NBC comedy series *The Good Place*.

29 The city I live in, Dundee, has made many contributions to cuisine, including orange marmalade, Dundee cake and, a few Christmases back, deep-fried mince pies.

30 I hope that I'll still make twenty-three years after my wife reads this paragraph.

31 For more on the New Testament's vision of what our eternal future looks like, see Tom Wright, *Surprised by Hope* (London: SPCK, 2007); or James Paul, *What on Earth Is Heaven?* (London: IVP, 2020).

from their eyes. There will be no more death' or mourning or crying or pain, for the old order of things has passed away. (Revelation 21:1–4)

Similarly to the Qur'an, the Bible sees our eternal dwelling place as representing a return to something like Eden. But whereas Allah in the Qur'an appears largely absent from both Eden and paradise, in the Bible we see Yahweh very present in both – walking and talking with Adam and Eve in Eden, and dwelling closely with his people in the new heavens and the new earth for eternity.

Running through all the Bible's descriptions of the afterlife is the promise of God's *presence*. In this life, Christians can enjoy a relationship with the God who graciously allows us to call him 'Father', but our vision of him is clouded. However, one day, the Bible promises, we will see clearly: 'For now we see only a reflection as in a mirror; then we shall see face to face. Now I know in part; then I shall know fully, even as I am fully known' (1 Corinthians 13:12).

Unlike in Islam, there need be no fear that one might lose one's place in paradise by sinning there, as Adam in the Qur'an did. For the Bible is also clear that Yahweh is at work within us, reforming and transforming Jesus' followers so that their very natures will be changed and sin will no longer affect them: 'being confident of this, that he who began a good work in you will carry it on to completion until the day of Christ Jesus' (Philippians 1:6).

Nor should Christians worry about boredom, about what happens after the one millionth deep-fried chocolate bar,[32] or bottle of the very best French wine, or romantic tête-à-tête with a heavenly houri, because the Bible offers us not an eternal conveyer belt of hedonic pleasure, but something far more profound: life with God in all its fullness. And because God is eternal and infinite, we can never

---

32 As the Canadian comedian Mike Myers once remarked: 'Most Scottish food is based on a dare.'

possibly outgrow him. The more we discover, the more there is to know:

> Then the angel showed me the river of the water of life, as clear as crystal, flowing from the throne of God and of the Lamb down the middle of the great street of the city. On each side of the river stood the tree of life, bearing twelve crops of fruit, yielding its fruit every month. And the leaves of the tree are for the healing of the nations. No longer will there be any curse. The throne of God and of the Lamb will be in the city, and his servants will serve him. They will see his face, and his name will be on their foreheads. There will be no more night. They will not need the light of a lamp or the light of the sun, for the Lord God will give them light. And they will reign for ever and ever.
>
> (Revelation 22:1–5)

Do all religions lead to god, as I am often asked? No. But more than that: not every religion *promises* to lead you to god. Some offer to lead you to oblivion, or a higher state of consciousness, and some, like Islam, claim to lead you to paradise. But only one that I know of dares to claim it can lead you to god – and that's Christianity.

Two different visions

Humanity is in a predicament: our lives and our world are entangled in sin, suffering and evil. When it comes to the solutions that Allah and Yahweh offer to those problems, there are profound differences – differences that are not illogical or inexplicable, but that flow from the different character of Yahweh and Allah in the Bible and the Qur'an.

For the Qur'an, Allah is a god who is not relational, or knowable by his human creations. He is not described as loving, and he certainly has never suffered on behalf of his creation. Allah created humans with an elevated position, vicegerents over creation, but ultimately they are only his slaves. Humans are weak and fallible, ignorant and disobedient, but Allah has provided a moral self-help programme which, if meticulously followed, can result in success and a reward: an eternity of food, drink and sex. But not an eternity in which Allah is present, because he was never a present-with-his-people kind of god in the first place.

For the Bible, Yahweh is utterly different. A god who *is* personal, knowable and relational. A god who *is* love, who *is* holy and who has always been willing to demonstrate that love through suffering. Human beings were created by Yahweh with a status above that of just servants; we are image bearers, designed for covenant relationship with him. Separated from that possibility by our sin and selfishness, Yahweh offered not self-help but *himself* – a rescue plan centred on his stepping into space and time and history. A rescue plan that leads not just to an eternity of more-of-the-same-but-slightly-better stuff in paradise but to a whole new creation, and an eternity dwelling with and growing ever closer to the God who made us and loves us.

Two very different *visions*. Two very different *gods*. And for the Bible, the way that someone sees best what Yahweh is like is to look at Jesus, the ultimate expression in space and time of who God is. However, many Christians are unaware that the Qur'an also talks about Jesus, where he is mentioned in about ninety verses. In the next chapter we will examine Jesus in both the Bible and the Qur'an and, as we do, discover why so many people have ended up confused about whether the God of the Qur'an and the God of the Bible are the same.

Key takeaways

- Concepts like 'salvation' and 'being saved' are alien to the Qur'an. Rather, what Allah has to offer is effectively a moral self-help programme: follow the provided guidance, keep

God's commands, work hard and maybe you will become one of the successful ones who will be rewarded.

- For the Qur'an, the reward for obedience is paradise – a place full of pleasures including wine, food and, for male believers, women. It is a place where every desire will be met. But what if you sin there (as Adam did)? Might you be cast out again? What if you get bored of a conveyor belt of pleasure stretching from here to eternity?

- By contrast, the Bible is clear that our brokenness and rebellion have separated us from God and, therefore, we need to rescued; we need a *saviour*, a term applied many times to Yahweh in the Old Testament and to Jesus in the New Testament. For the Bible, God's rescue plan is based on the provision of a sacrifice – one who dies in our place – with the Old Testament sacrificial system pointing forward to Jesus' once-for-all perfect sacrifice for us.

- The Bible's offer of salvation through Jesus promises not just forgiveness for our wrongdoing but also healing of our broken nature – indeed, the promise of a whole new nature. And the hope of an eternity living in a renewed heaven and earth, enjoying the close presence of God for ever.

8

The misfit Messiah

How putting Jesus in his place
helps us see God clearly

As a former Londoner, one of my favourite pastimes when I visit the city of my birth is to walk the banks of the River Thames. Particularly along the riverside in the borough of Southwark, there are many impressive sights to see: everything from London Bridge to the Tate Modern gallery, from the Shard to HMS *Belfast*. But the highlight for me is the Globe Theatre, an authentic reconstruction of Shakespeare's original Elizabethan playhouse which was destroyed by Puritans in the seventeenth century (taking 'theatre criticism' to a whole new level).

Imagine that you manage to get hold of tickets for the opening night's performance of an innovative new production of *Macbeth* at the Globe Theatre. Everything begins well and you are having a wonderful time watching the tale of murder and intrigue (it's almost as bloodthirsty as watching the BBC Parliament channel). Eventually the curtain goes down on Act 4 and you wander off to the theatre's stylish café for a cappuccino and a piece of overpriced chocolate cake, returning just in time to see the curtain go up on Act 5.

But something isn't quite right. Now the stage is full of androids and lasers, flashing lights, dancers, explosions and all manner of special effects. It's noisy and remarkably impressive, but you're confused. For sure, there's a robot dog who keeps getting under everybody's feet, leading to cries of 'Out, damned Spot!', an animatronic alien called 'Duncan', a spaceship called the 'USS *Dunsinane*' and lots of talk of a secret weapon called 'The Birnam

Wood of Doom', but for all of that, this is obviously *not* the same story. It may use the same names as Shakespeare's play; it may even be fun and exciting in a zany sci-fi way; but it clearly does not belong as Act 5 of *Macbeth*. Next time you watch Shakespeare, you think to yourself, as you head home through the darkening streets, you'll try something lighter, maybe *Love's Labour's Won*.

Borrowing versus inheritance

Just because one story uses the same names and characters as another story, it does not automatically mean that the two stories are related. Rather, we must discern whether these elements have been *borrowed* or whether they have been *inherited*.

To understand the difference between inheritance and borrowing, consider an architectural example. One of my favourite buildings is York Minster, arguably the finest cathedral in England. Its history is fascinating: the beautiful Norman church and later cathedral were built on top of an older Saxon church, the medieval building growing as the older church was extended and upgraded. But underpinning the Saxon church is something even more ancient: the ruins of a Roman military barracks. Take the tour of the crypt and you can descend through layers of history, right down to the Roman rubble in the foundations.

But there is a key difference between the Roman, Saxon and Norman ruins. As York Minster expanded, it grew organically out of the older churches as they were extended and developed. But the Roman ruins in the crypt? Certainly, Roman stone was used, as it was handy for the Saxon church builders to have tons of dressed stone lying around doing nothing.[1] But the Saxons used the Roman material purely as building blocks – there is no continuity between the Roman ruins and the church.

---

1 'Look what the Romans have done for us!'

In other words, the medieval York Minster *inherited* from the Norman and Saxon churches, whereas it *borrowed* from the Roman barracks, repurposing the stones and dumping them unceremoniously into the foundations of the new construction.

In his book *The Qur'an and Its Biblical Reflexes*, Mark Durie offers another example that can help us understand the difference between inheritance and borrowing, this time from language. When two languages derive from a common source, they share not just words in common but also deeply related structures. For example, consider the words for 'mouse' in English, Icelandic and German.[2] In English, the singular is 'mouse' and the plural 'mice'; in Icelandic it's *mús/mýs*; and in German *Maus/Mäuse*. Notice how the singular and plural forms all show the same pattern: an internal variation in the vowel. This shared structural feature is a clue that these languages derive from a common source, that is, they have a shared *inheritance*.

By contrast, borrowing is typically highly destructive. Consider the word 'juggernaut', borrowed by the English language from Sanskrit via Hindi. It was originally Jagannatha, a Sanskrit name for a Hindu god, whose worship involved the crushing of devotees beneath the wheels of enormous chariots. But that context was entirely lost when English destructively borrowed the term.

The Qur'an and the Bible: borrowing or inheritance?

A reader of the Qur'an who is also familiar with the Bible soon notices that the Qur'an frequently refers to biblical stories and characters. Among the characters who turn up on the pages of the Qur'an,[3] we can find Aaron, Abraham, Adam, David, Elijah,

---

2 Mark Durie, *The Qur'an and Its Biblical Reflexes: Investigations into the genesis of a religion* (Lanham, MD: Lexington Books, 2018), p. xl.

3 Many of these have Arabized names; for example, Aaron is Harun, Elijah is Elias, and Jonah is Yunus.

Elisha, Ezra, Gabriel, Goliath, Isaac, Ishmael, Jacob, Jesus, John, Jonah, Joseph, Lot, Mary, Moses, Noah, Pharaoh, Saul, Solomon and Zechariah.

As well as names, biblical ideas and concepts turn up: everything from monotheism to worship, idolatry to sin, law to scripture. No wonder that some people, glancing at this phenomenon, have concluded the Qur'an must be a sequel to the Bible, and Islam the third act of the play after Judaism and Christianity.

But has the Qur'an inherited these ideas and concepts from the Bible or has it borrowed them? I want to suggest that the Qur'an's theology does not grow organically from the Bible but rather – like the Roman foundations of York Minster, the word 'juggernaut' or the sci-fi version of *Macbeth* – the Qur'an has *borrowed*, extensively and destructively, losing context and meaning in the process. The result is much confusion, not least about God, his nature and his identity. How can we demonstrate my claim that the Qur'an has borrowed rather than inherited? The example par excellence that proves it is Jesus.

Jesus in the Qur'an

While Jesus stands at the centre of the Christian faith, many people are unaware that he is also an important figure in Islam. I remember being surprised the first time a Muslim friend announced: 'I love Jesus as much as you do.' Why was my friend so drawn to Jesus? Simply because the Qur'an is fascinated by him, discussing Jesus in roughly ninety verses and mentioning him by name in twenty-five verses, where it uses an Arabized version of his name, Isa.[4] A good place to get an overview of the qur'anic Jesus is with this verse from the Qur'an's fifth sura, where his ministry is summarized:

---

4   Q. 2:87, 136, 253; 3:45, 52, 55, 59, 84; 4:157, 163, 171; 5:46, 78, 110, 112, 114, 116; 6:85; 19:34; 33:7; 42:13; 43:63; 57:27; 61:6, 14.

(Remember) when God said, 'Jesus, son of Mary! Remember My blessing on you and on your mother, when I supported you with the holy spirit, (and) you spoke to the people (while you were still) in the cradle, and in adulthood. And when I taught you the Book and the wisdom, and the Torah and the Gospel. And when you created the form of a bird from clay by My permission, and you breathed into it, and it became a bird by My permission, and you healed the blind and the leper by My permission. And when you brought forth the dead by My permission, and when I restrained the Sons of Israel from (violence against) you. When you brought them the clear signs, those among them who had disbelieved said, "This is nothing but clear magic."'

(Q. 5:110)

Miracles such as healing the blind and the leprous, or raising the dead, are familiar to readers of the Bible, while references to Jesus speaking in the cradle and bringing a clay bird to life are drawn from later legendary stories that developed in the centuries after the Bible, such as those found in the *Infancy Gospel of Thomas* and the *Gospel of Pseudo-Matthew*.[5] As Muslim scholar Shabir Ally explains, the Qur'an draws from legends and fables as well as the biographical accounts of Jesus in the New Testament,[6] because 'history' is not its chief concern: 'The Qur'an is not here to teach people history . . . the Qur'an is calling people back to God with these stories.'[7]

Elsewhere in the Qur'an, we read of Jesus' miraculous virgin birth; indeed, the Qur'an is so fascinated by this story that it retells it twice,[8]

---

5 See Gabriel Said Reynolds, *The Qur'ān and the Bible: Text and commentary* (New Haven, CT: Yale University Press, 2018), pp. 215–216.

6 On the biblical Gospels as eyewitness-based biographies, see Richard Bauckham, *Jesus and the Eyewitnesses: The Gospels as eyewitness testimony*, 2nd edn (Grand Rapids, MI: Eerdmans, 2017).

7 Shabir made this comment during a dialogue/debate with David Wood: watch the video of their interaction at <www.youtube.com/watch?v=n5qSwcYEJz8>.

8 Q. 3:42–48 and Q. 19:16–34.

with some significant differences between the two accounts.[9] Here, to give us a flavour, are three verses from one of those accounts:

When the angels said, 'Mary! Surely God gives you good news of a word from Him: his name is the Messiah, Jesus, son of Mary, eminent in this world and the Hereafter, and one of those brought near. He will speak to the people (while he is still) in the cradle and in adulthood, and (he will be) one of the righteous.' She said, 'My Lord, how shall I have a child, when no man has touched me?' He said, 'So (it will be)! God creates whatever He pleases. When He decrees something, He simply says to it, "Be!" and it is.'
(Q. 3:45–47)

The Qur'an also applies some very lofty titles to Jesus: he is described as the 'Messiah' (Q. 4:172), as a 'Word from God' (see Q. 3:45) and a 'Spirit from God' (see Q. 4:171). In addition, it reserves a special role for Jesus at the end of history: 'And (Jesus) shall be a Sign (for the coming of) the Hour (of Judgment): therefore have no doubt about the (Hour), but follow ye Me: this is a Straight Way' (Q. 43:61). Later Islamic tradition would greatly expand this future role for Jesus, with many hadith explaining how he will return at the end of time to fight the Antichrist, *al-Dajjal*:

It would be at this very time that Allah would send Jesus, son of Mary, and he will descend at the white minaret in the eastern side of Damascus wearing two garments lightly dyed with saffron and placing his hands on the wings of two Angels. When he would lower his head, there would fall beads of perspiration from his head, and when he would raise it up, beads like pearls would scatter from it. Every non-believer who would smell

9   For example, in Q. 3:42 it is the angels (plural) who come to Mary, while in Q. 19:17 it is Allah's spirit who takes 'the form of a human' and appears to her.

the odor of his self would die and his breath would reach as far as he would be able to see. He would then search for him [*al-Dajjal*, the Antichrist] until he would catch hold of him at the gate of Ludd [a village near Jerusalem] and would kill him. Then a people whom Allah had protected would come to Jesus, son of Mary, and he would wipe their faces and would inform them of their ranks in Paradise . . .

(Sahih Muslim 2937)

Despite his amazing birth, tremendous miracles and significant titles, the Qur'an is exceedingly keen to cut Jesus down to size. For example, his place in the prophetic line as just-another-prophet is frequently stressed:

Say: 'We believe in God, and what has been sent down on us, and what has been sent down on Abraham, and Ishmael, and Isaac, and Jacob, and the tribes, and what was given to Moses, and Jesus, and the prophets from their Lord. We make no distinction between any of them, and to Him we submit.'
(Q. 3:84)

The Qur'an also regularly asserts Jesus' humanity, attacking the Christian belief in his divinity: 'Surely the likeness of Jesus is, with God, as the likeness of Adam. He created him from dust, (and) then He said to him, "Be!" and he was' (Q. 3:59).

Then, most notoriously of all, the Qur'an denies the central claim of the Bible (and of first-century history) that Jesus was crucified: '[The Jews say:] "Surely we killed the Messiah, Jesus, son of Mary, the messenger of God" – yet they did not kill him, nor did they crucify him, but it (only) seemed like (that) to them' (Q. 4:157).[10]

---

10 Most Muslim scholars have understood this verse to imply that Allah made somebody else look like Jesus; that substitute was then killed in Jesus' place, thereby allowing Jesus to trick people into thinking he had risen from the dead.

This polemical focus makes the qur'anic Jesus unique, for no other prophet in the Qur'an is so entangled in controversy. As Muslim scholar Tarif Khalidi acknowledges: 'In sum, the Qur'anic Jesus, unlike any other prophet, is embroiled in polemic . . . [He] is in fact an argument addressed to his more wayward followers.'[11]

Another Muslim scholar, Shabbir Akhtar of the University of Oxford, agrees that a key concern of the Qur'an is to critique Christian ideas about Jesus. In contrast to the Bible, Akhtar claims that the Qur'an is much more down to earth: 'Its view of Jesus is modest in comparison with the New Testament's appraisal which the Qur'an dismisses as zealous excess.'[12] Yet Akhtar is stretching things considerably, for to call the Qur'an's presentation of Jesus 'modest' is rather like describing the protagonist in a superhero movie as 'slightly out of the ordinary'. The Qur'an has a standard biography that it woodenly applies to its prophets: a qur'anic prophet is a solitary man, sent to one people, who is rejected; his people are then destroyed, and the prophet is rescued. The Qur'an attempts to squeeze most of the biblical prophets whose stories it retells into this mould.

But not Jesus.

Jesus stands out, head and shoulders above every other qur'anic prophet. He is born miraculously of a virgin. He performs a galaxy of miracles, in both childhood and adulthood; no other prophet (certainly not Muhammad) did anything like them. He is given incredible titles ('Word of God'; 'Spirit of God') that are full of significance. Jesus is also called 'the Messiah', a title that gave later Muslim scholars huge problems, as the Qur'an nowhere explains its meaning.[13] Finally, Jesus' role on the day of judgment, hinted at in

---

11 Tarif Khalidi, *The Muslim Jesus: Sayings and stories in Islamic literature* (Cambridge, MA: Harvard University Press, 2001), pp. 12, 16.

12 Shabbir Akhtar, 'Finding and following Jesus: the Muslim claim to the Messiah', *Yaqeen Institute for Islamic Research* (2018), p. 7.

13 The fourteenth-century Iranian Muslim scholar al-Firuzabadi lists over fifty interpretations of the word 'Messiah', including 'flat-footed', because Jesus walked about preaching so much his feet were flat. See Edward William Lane, *An Arabic-English Lexicon* (London: Williams & Norgate, 1863), '*masīḥ*', p. 2714.

the Qur'an and enormously expanded in later Islam, also looks rather peculiar, for while Islam claims that *Muhammad* was the final prophet, it is the qur'anic *Jesus* who will return at the end of history.

For Shabbir Akhtar to describe the Qur'an's portrayal of Jesus as 'modest' is not simply to play fast and loose; it's more like unscrewing all the wheel nuts and taking a Bugatti Veyron for a 200-mile-per-hour sprint around the Nürburgring. The problem is that Jesus simply doesn't fit into Islam. The qur'anic Jesus is a bizarre oddity, borrowed from elsewhere and then forced into the Qur'an, rather like a five-year-old child hammering on the wrong jigsaw piece in the hope it will fit if thumped hard enough.

Borrowing like this invariably destroys the context and often sows confusion in the process. The Jesus of the Qur'an has been borrowed from the Bible and makes about as much sense in the Qur'an as, say, Gandalf might, if borrowed from *The Lord of the Rings* and parachuted into the pages of *Pride and Prejudice*:

'Why, Mr Darcy, you're late,' exclaimed Elizabeth, fluttering her fan coquettishly.

'It's Gandalf to you, young lady,' harrumphed Gandalf, helping himself to a teacake. 'Besides which, a wizard is never late; nor is he early. He arrives precisely when the buffet is about to begin.'

'Nevertheless, my precious,' Elizabeth continued, 'it is a truth universally acknowledged that a wizard in possession of a good beard must be in want of a shave.'

'Enough of this small talk,' said Gandalf. 'Shall we amuse ourselves, Miss Bennet, with a game of cards?'

'I think I'll pass, Mr Gandalf. I much prefer reading. Have you seen Mr Tolkien's latest?'

'Pass? Pass! You cannot pass! I am a servant of the Secret Fire, wielder of the flame of Anor. You cannot pass. And besides, I'm a wizard when it comes to whist.'

Just as Gandalf does not belong in the world of *Pride and Prejudice* (although he might liven things up a bit), so Jesus does not belong in the Qur'an and Islam. He has been borrowed, ripped from his home habitat, and even though the Qur'an does its utmost to squeeze him into its theology, Jesus simply refuses to fit.

Putting Jesus in his place

However, Jesus does fit into Christianity and into the Bible where, as one reads the New Testament, it is made abundantly clear that he is far more than a prophet, more than a mere messenger, because Jesus' main function is to reveal God to us. So much confusion about God comes because we often think of God as distant and unknowable and we are tempted to project our very human ideas of what he is like on to him. But as Tom Wright points out:

> The whole New Testament, in fact, stands against this approach. Hebrews, for example, describes Jesus as 'the radiance of God's glory and the exact representation of his being' (Hebrews 1:3). The answer to the question, 'Who is God?', from a [biblical] standpoint, is 'Look at Jesus'.[14]

From the Bible's perspective, if you get Jesus wrong, you risk misunderstanding God. Just as if I put a damaged or dirty lens on to my camera I won't be able to see clearly the mountain I am trying to photograph, so if Jesus is not in his proper place, we won't be able to see God clearly.

I appreciate that for my Muslim friends this is a big stumbling block. Back in my days at Speakers' Corner, most of the questions I was asked by Muslims concerned Jesus – in particular, why do

---

14 Tom Wright, 'God with us: a paradigm for life during the pandemic', in Luke Cawley and Kristi Mair (eds.), *Healthy Faith and the Coronavirus Crisis: Thriving in the COVID-19 pandemic* (London: IVP, 2020), pp. 263–267, citing p. 264.

Christians believe he is more than a man, that he is God's own Son, not just worthy of listening to but also worthy of our worship?

The question of worship is a good place to begin because it is worship that, throughout two thousand years of history, has marked out Christians as being, well, Christian. It has long been noted by historians that wherever one looks in ancient history, every Christian group that we know of – whether more mainstream or more at the fruit-and-nut end of the theological spectrum – every Christian group *worshipped* Jesus.

Even the enemies of the early church were well aware of this. In AD 112 in Bithynia (in modern-day Turkey), the Roman governor, Pliny the Younger,[15] was having trouble with Christians who were refusing to worship the emperor. Having tried cajoling, threats and even the offer of tickets to the opening night of *Macbeth*, Pliny was at his wits' end and wrote to the emperor Trajan for advice. His letter gives a fascinating snapshot into how early Christians were seen by their Roman contemporaries. Pliny remarks that Christians were 'accustomed to meet on a fixed day before dawn and sing responsively a hymn *to Christ as to a god*'.[16]

Pliny's letter reveals that within eighty years of the crucifixion and resurrection, not only had Christianity spread widely across the Roman Empire but also Christians were well known for the fact that they worshipped Jesus.

This is fascinating because Christianity began as an offshoot of Judaism. Most of the first Christians were Jewish, and in Judaism it was worship that marked out God from everything else. The rule was simple: God was worshipped. Everything else – rocks, sacred springs, rubber chickens, emperors – was not. For Jews, Yahweh was, uniquely, the creator and ruler of everything, and because of that, he alone was worthy of worship. Richard Bauckham,

---

15 Not to be confused with his lesser-known brothers, Pliny the Even Younger and Pliny the Young-but-Not-Quite-as-Young-as-Pliny-the-Younger.

16 Pliny, *Letters* 10.96, my emphasis.

Emeritus Professor at St Andrew's University in Scotland, writes: 'In Jewish monotheism, monolatry, the exclusive worship of the one God . . . most clearly signalled the distinction between God and all other reality. God must be worshipped; no other being may be worshipped.'[17]

Not merely did every Christian group we know of in history worship Jesus; we likewise find that on virtually every page of the New Testament documents, writings that are thoroughly Jewish in their thinking and theology, Jesus is included in the identity of God through worship. For example, in one of the latest New Testament books, Revelation, Jesus is depicted as a lamb, standing on God's throne and receiving worship.[18] It is a similar picture in the book of Hebrews, where Jesus is depicted receiving the worship of angels: 'when God brings his firstborn into the world, he says: "Let all God's angels worship him"' (Hebrews 1:6–7).

In Philippians 2, there lies preserved an incredibly early Christian hymn, which portrays Jesus as receiving worship and adoration:

That at the name of Jesus every knee should bow,
    in heaven and on earth and under the earth,
and every tongue confess that Jesus Christ is Lord,
    to the glory of God the Father.
(Philippians 2:10–11 NIV 1984)

What is particularly striking is that those words are quoted from the Old Testament book of Isaiah, where they were originally applied to Yahweh.[19] The hymn in Philippians thus boldly proclaims that Isaiah's ancient vision of every nation worshipping Yahweh is fulfilled when people worship Jesus.

---

17 Richard Bauckham, *God Crucified: Monotheism and Christology in the New Testament* (Carlisle: Paternoster Press, 1998), p. 13.

18 Revelation 5:6; 7:9–10.

19 Isaiah 45:23.

These three examples are drawn from a collection of hundreds, for every New Testament document, on page after page, contains similar themes. The worship of Jesus that we saw in early Christianity begins in the Bible itself.

But as well as more direct examples of worship, there are hundreds of indirect examples. Time after time, Christians in the New Testament, when invoking the name of Jesus, 'call on the name of the Lord' – a phrase that in the Old Testament exclusively applied to Yahweh.[20] Baptism, the entrance rite to early Christianity whereby converts were plunged into water, was also carried out 'in the name of Jesus'.[21] Also in the early church's prayer life, Jesus' name was frequently invoked, including in exorcisms when evil spirits were cast out by the power of his name.[22]

In short, all across the New Testament and early Christianity we see Christians using the name of Jesus in the way that God's name was used in Judaism, and Jesus receiving the kind of worship that was uniquely directed to God in the Old Testament. Furthermore, Jesus is portrayed in the New Testament as doing and accomplishing what, in the Old Testament, Yahweh had promised he would do. Most notably, it is God alone who is 'saviour', says the Old Testament in over forty passages.[23] But in the New Testament, it is Jesus who carries out this role; Jesus himself, at the Last Supper, directly connects what he is about to do through his death and resurrection with what God did through the exodus in the Old Testament.[24]

Professor Larry Hurtado, who has written extensively on Jesus' place in early Christianity, states:

---

20 See e.g. Acts 9:14, 21; 1 Corinthians 1:2; compare e.g. 1 Chronicles 16:8; Psalms 105:1; 116:13.

21 See e.g. Matthew 28:19; Acts 2:38; 8:16; 10:48; 19:4; Romans 6:3; 1 Corinthians 1:13; Galatians 3:27.

22 See e.g. Ephesians 5:20; James 5:14; Acts 3:6; 16:18; 19:13–16.

23 For example, Isaiah 43:11.

24 See e.g. Mark 14:12–26; compare 1 Corinthians 10:23–26.

In historical terms we may refer to a veritable 'big bang', an explosively rapid and impressively substantial christological development in the earliest stage of the Christian movement . . . At an astonishingly early point basic convictions about Jesus that amount to treating him as divine had become widely shared in various Christian circles.[25]

So where does all of this come from? From where did Christians get the idea that Jesus was to be worshipped as God? If it was just one obscure Christian group who practised this, we could write them off as an oddity, concluding that's what comes of too many late-night prayer meetings and goat's cheese soufflés. But we see this *everywhere*: on every page of the New Testament and in every Christian group we know of.

We really only have two choices. Either Jesus was the most incompetent religious teacher in history, or all of this goes back to Jesus himself.

If we look at the first possibility, it means that Jesus was so comically bad at teaching, it would have been better had he not taken it up at all, but pursued a different career, perhaps accountancy. Despite not intending to, somehow Jesus ended up accidentally conveying to his followers that the most important thing was to worship him: what a total disaster! That's the first possibility: Jesus was a spectacular failure.

But the second possibility is that Jesus taught precisely this, and taught it frequently and deliberately. I want to suggest that he did so. That by far the best explanation for what we see in the New Testament and in the practice of Christians throughout two thousand years of history is that Jesus taught – through his words and his actions – that he was divine. If that is the case, then no matter how much it may

---

25 See Larry W. Hurtado, *Lord Jesus Christ: Devotion to Jesus in earliest Christianity* (Grand Rapids, MI: Eerdmans, 2003), p. 135.

disturb us, we need to follow the evidence where it leads and either take Jesus at his word, or turn and walk away.[26]

Who did Jesus think he was?

The first clue to Jesus' self-identity concerns his attitude to the Old Testament. Despite this being sacred scripture to the Jewish people, Jesus' treatment of it is fascinating. In his famous 'Sermon on the Mount' there are a number of occasions where Jesus says, 'You have heard that it was said . . .', quotes the Old Testament, and then proceeds to put his *own* words on a par with or above it ('but *I* say to you . . .').[27] I sometimes ask Muslim friends what they would think if next Friday they went to the mosque, only to hear the imam say, 'The Qur'an says this, but I say to you something else.' I suspect such an approach would be a career-ending piece of innovation. Yet Jesus regularly does it, leading the renowned Jewish scholar Jacob Neusner to remark that Jesus' attitude to Torah made him want to ask, 'Who do you think you are? God?'[28]

A second clue comes from Jesus' approach to forgiveness. In the Gospel of Mark there is a fascinating story where Jesus forgives a man's sins, causing a crisis for the religious leaders, who protest, 'Why does this fellow talk like that? He's blaspheming! Who can forgive sins but God alone?' Jesus' response is striking:

> Immediately Jesus knew in his spirit that this was what they were thinking in their hearts, and he said to them, 'Why are you thinking these things? Which is easier: to say to this

---

26 In what follows, we just scratch the surface of a mountain of evidence. For a much more thorough treatment, I can highly recommend Robert Bowman and J. Ed Komoszewski, *Putting Jesus in His Place: The case for the deity of Christ* (Grand Rapids, MI: Kregel, 2007).

27 See e.g. Matthew 5:21–48.

28 Cited in N. T. Wright, 'The biblical formation of a doctrine of Christ', in Donald Armstrong (ed.), *Who Do You Say That I Am? Christology and the church* (Grand Rapids, MI: Eerdmans, 1999), pp. 47–68, citing p. 63.

paralysed man, "Your sins are forgiven," or to say, "Get up, take your mat and walk"? But I want you to know that the Son of Man [Jesus' favourite title for himself] has authority on earth to forgive sins.' So he said to the man, 'I tell you, get up, take your mat and go home.' He got up, took his mat and walked out in full view of them all.

(Mark 2:7–12)

There are actually two problems here. The first is the one the religious leaders identify, namely that forgiving sin is God's prerogative. But the second is that Judaism *had* a place for forgiveness, namely the temple in Jerusalem. If you sinned, you were supposed to go there and offer your sacrifice. As N. T. Wright remarks: 'Judaism had two great incarnational symbols, Temple and Torah: Jesus seems to have believed it was his vocation to upstage the one and outflank the other.'[29]

A third central religious symbol in the Judaism of Jesus' time was the Jewish holy day, the sabbath, and here again we see Jesus using it to express his identity. Further on in Mark's Gospel, Jesus has another confrontation with the religious leaders, the Pharisees, who object to his disciples picking grain on the sabbath. At the climax of the confrontation, Jesus announces: 'So the Son of Man is Lord even of the Sabbath' (Mark 2:28).

It is difficult to overstate how important the sabbath was to Judaism. Faithful Jews believed it was sacred time, the sabbath being an institution that God himself had set up at the very beginning of creation.[30] Thus for Jesus to claim lordship over the sabbath was tantamount to him proclaiming: 'I am the Lord of Space and Time.' Indeed, it is no surprise that later in the Gospels, Jesus' attitude to the sabbath is one reason for the attempt by the religious authorities to kill him: 'For this reason they tried all the more to kill him; not

---

29 Wright, 'The biblical formation of a doctrine of Christ', p. 64.
30 See Genesis 2:2–3; Exodus 20:8–11.

only was he breaking the Sabbath, but he was even calling God his own Father, making himself equal with God' (John 5:18).

Next we have Jesus' attitude to his own name. Rather than introduce his teaching in the way the Old Testament prophets did, by announcing, 'The Lord says to you . . .', Jesus preferred to simply begin, 'I say to you . . .'[31] He also taught his followers to pray in his name, and promised that when they gathered together in his name, his presence would be with them.[32]

This attitude to his name and identity is further reinforced by Jesus' view about what his miracles revealed. The Gospels are full of stories of Jesus' miracles, from healings to exorcisms to the reviving of the dead. And on several occasions, Jesus unpacks what he thinks they signify. For example, when John the Baptist is languishing in prison and beginning to doubt who Jesus is, John sends messengers to Jesus to ask whether he is indeed the Messiah. Jesus replies:

Go back and report to John what you have seen and heard: the blind receive sight, the lame walk, those who have leprosy are cleansed, the deaf hear, the dead are raised, and the good news is proclaimed to the poor.
(Luke 7:22)

Jesus is quoting here from Isaiah 61 in order to show how the kind of miracles he is doing are *messianic* miracles, validating his identity as Messiah. In keeping with this, Jesus believed that all the prophets and the law pointed forward, prophesying about events up to the time of John the Baptist, whose role was to pave the way for Jesus. Jesus himself said, 'All the Prophets and the Law prophesied until John' (Matthew 11:13). This was actually a common belief in Judaism;

---

31 Among dozens of occurrences, see e.g. Matthew 5:18; Mark 9:41; Luke 4:24; John 3:3.
32 See e.g. Matthew 18:5, 20; 24:5; Mark 9:37, 39; 13:6; Luke 9:48; 21:8; John 14:13, 14, 26; 15:16; 16:23, 24, 26.

as the Jewish Talmud explains it: 'All prophets prophesied only for the days of the Messiah.'[33]

We saw earlier how the qur'anic Jesus, despite bearing the title 'Messiah', has been flattened into just another prophet. But this simply doesn't work: the Messiah is supposed to come at the *end* of the prophetic line, not part-way through it. And so I have often pointed out to Muslim friends that if Jesus *was* the Messiah, as the Qur'an teaches, then Muhammad cannot be a prophet – for the Messiah is the one *to whom every other prophet points*.

But Jesus went even further than simply saying, 'These miracles show I am the Messiah'; he also interpreted the miracles as proof of his divine identity. For example, speaking of his exorcisms, Jesus proclaimed: 'If I drive out demons by the finger of God, then the kingdom of God has come upon you' (Luke 11:20). Jesus drew that little phrase, 'the finger of God', from the Old Testament, where it is used, most significantly, to describe Yahweh's writing of the Ten Commandments on the two stone tablets that he gave to Moses on top of Mount Sinai.[34] It is a powerful Old Testament phrase used to describe God acting directly, and Jesus says this is what he is doing when he performs his miracles.

Finally, as we consider who Jesus thought himself to be, we come to his favourite title for himself: 'the Son of Man'.[35] That title comes from the Old Testament, from Daniel 7, where 'one like a son of man' is enthroned beside God in heaven:

In my vision at night I looked, and there before me was one like a son of man, coming with the clouds of heaven. He approached the Ancient of Days and was led into his presence. He was given authority, glory and sovereign power; all nations and peoples of every language worshipped him. His dominion is

---

33 Babylonian Talmud, *Tractate Sanhedrin*, folio 99a.

34 Exodus 31:18; Deuteronomy 9:10.

35 The title occurs almost sixty times in the Gospels, always in the speech of Jesus.

an everlasting dominion that will not pass away, and his kingdom is one that will never be destroyed.

(Daniel 7:13–14)

At the end of his public ministry, as Jesus stands before Caiaphas the
high priest, on trial for his life, Caiaphas demands to know who on
earth Jesus thinks he is: 'The high priest asked him, "Are you the
Messiah, the Son of the Blessed One?"' (Mark 14:61). This was the
moment at which Jesus, had he wished, could have replied, 'No, it's
all been a mistake.' But instead he quotes the passage above from
Daniel 7 to the high priest, who, understanding full well what that
meant, completely and totally loses it: 'The high priest tore his
clothes. "Why do we need any more witnesses?" he asked. "You have
heard the blasphemy. What do you think?" They all condemned him
as worthy of death' (Mark 14:63–64).

During a dialogue in Toronto with Muslim scholar Shabir Ally on
the subject of Jesus' identity, I brought up this passage, and Shabir's
reply was that the high priest had simply misunderstood Jesus, who
had not meant to imply any kind of divine identity. I remember
responding, 'Shabir, you're on trial, before a man with the power to
condemn you to death for blasphemy. He asks if you think you're the
Son of the Blessed One, of Yahweh himself. You have one chance and
one chance only to get this answer right. Think carefully. Do you say
"No", or do you instead choose to quote Daniel 7?'

Shabir was stuck between a rock and hard place. For either one
has to admit that Jesus was *completely* insane, unwittingly goading
Caiaphas into executing him, and in a kinder, gentler age would
have been a candidate for a room with padded walls and one of
those lovely comfortable jackets with the sleeves that helpfully
buckle up at the back. Or one must conclude that Jesus knew
entirely what he was doing, namely telling the truth – even when
he knew it would cost him his life, as he had planned all along. For
as Jesus had earlier said: 'even the Son of Man did not come to be

served, but to serve, and to give his life as a ransom for many'
(Mark 10:45).

Jesus helps us see God clearly

As we reflect on what Jesus said, taught and claimed, we are faced
with just one of three possibilities: either Jesus was stark raving mad;
or he was an arrogant, lying self-aggrandizer; or he was, in fact, who
he claimed to be. There does not seem to be any fourth possibility,
certainly not a just-a-misunderstood-prophet option. As the famous
New Testament scholar Raymond Brown concluded, after a lifetime
of studying the biblical texts: 'The idea that [Jesus] was divine I find
on most gospel pages.'[36]

Three days after Jesus' execution by crucifixion, when he rose
bodily from the grave, his followers took that to be a vindication of
everything he had claimed about himself.[37] Had Jesus remained in
the tomb, he would have been a dead blasphemer; but when he rose
from the dead, it was divine confirmation of everything he had said.
No wonder that Christians immediately began to worship Jesus,
including him in the identity of Yahweh, the God of the Old
Testament, and doing so in thoroughly Jewish ways! As Richard
Bauckham remarks:

> [T]he highest possible Christology, the inclusion of Jesus in the
> unique divine identity, was central to the faith of the early
> church even before any of the New Testament writings were
> written, since it occurs in all of them . . . The New Testament
> writers did not see their Jewish monotheistic heritage as a

---

36 Raymond Brown, 'Did Jesus know he was God?', *Biblical Theology Bulletin* 15 (1985),
pp. 74–79, citing p. 77.
37 We don't have time here to review the substantial historical evidence for Jesus' resurrection. For a brief overview, watch my video 'What Is the Evidence for the Resurrection?',
<www.solas-cpc.org/what-is-the-evidence-for-the-resurrection-andy-bannister>; or for
more detail, read Gary R. Habermas and Michael R. Licona, *The Case for the Resurrection
of Jesus* (Grand Rapids, MI: Kregel, 2004).

problem, rather they used its resources extensively in order precisely to include Jesus in the divine identity.[38]

Why does any of this matter? It matters tremendously because Jesus' entire ministry was about revealing God to us. As we have seen, people throw the word 'god' around very loosely, but not all conceptions of god are the same. This can then become a problem when we discuss Jesus, for when people ask 'Is Jesus god?' they usually think they know what 'god' means, then see if Jesus fits that concept. But that doesn't work; for example, if you take Allah, the God of the Qur'an, and ask 'Is Jesus Allah?', it gets precisely nowhere. For as N. T. Wright points out:

> If you start with the New Age gods-from-below, or for that matter the gods of ancient paganism [or the God of the Qur'an], and ask what would happen if such a god were to become human, you would end up with a figure very different from the one in the Gospels. But if you start with the God of Genesis, the God of the Exodus, of Isaiah, of creation and covenant, of the Psalms, and ask what that God might look like, were he to become human, you will find that he might look very like Jesus of Nazareth.[39]

If you want to know what Yahweh, the God of the Bible is like, look at Jesus. All the characteristics of God's identity are brought into clearer, sharper focus through the lens of Jesus' life, death and resurrection.

The Qur'an, however, has entirely misunderstood Jesus. As it has borrowed him, it has ripped Jesus from his context and jammed him into a new story, losing much in the process. But Jesus is not alone in having the Qur'an do this to him, for in a sense the Qur'an has

---

38 Bauckham, *God Crucified*, p. 27.

39 Wright, 'The biblical formation of a doctrine of Christ', p. 65.

simply done with Jesus what it has done with God – turning him into a moralizer, one who dispenses advice and wisdom, one who tells us how to live (and in the case of Jesus, models that for us), but who offers us no help, no rescue and certainly no power to live differently.

Yet, despite the Qur'an's attempt at remodelling him, the qur'anic Jesus remains far too big for his Islamic boots, straining to burst out of the constraints of the story into which the Qur'an has attempted to shoehorn him. The Australian scholar Richard Shumack points this out at the end of his book *Jesus through Muslim Eyes*:

> In Islam, [Jesus] is an extraordinary discovery, but he doesn't feel properly located there. He seems dislocated from his natural 'messianic' habitat. That habitat is Christianity. There, his origins fit, his miracles belong, his teaching coheres, and he makes sense of Jewish prophecy . . . In the end, in Islam, Jesus is striking, but dislocated. In Christianity, he is glorious, and religiously at home.[40]

The Qur'an's dislocation of Jesus has tremendous implications, because if you get Jesus wrong, there's a very good chance you will get God wrong. The God of the Bible is relational, knowable, holy, loving, and has suffered. He places tremendous value on his human creations because he created us in his image and designed us for relationship with him. Grieved by our rebellion, sinfulness and brokenness, he did not leave us to our fate but offered a rescue plan – a way back into friendship with him. All these aspects and actions of Yahweh, the God of the Bible, are brought into sharp focus through Jesus.

But of all the aspects of Yahweh's nature and character, the one that the Bible consistently and repeatedly points to as powerfully

---

40 Richard Shumack, *Jesus through Muslim Eyes* (London: SPCK, 2020), p. 102.

displayed in Jesus is Yahweh's nature as a God of love. There is something about love that must be shown through action; words are not enough. Anybody can *say* 'I love you', but their words are largely meaningless unless that love is also *demonstrated*. So, what about God's love? Well, says the Bible, if you want to know whether God is love – indeed more profoundly, if you want to know for sure if God loves *you*, brokenness and all – then look at Jesus: 'God demonstrates his own love for us in this: while we were still sinners, Christ died for us' (Romans 5:8).

It is also love that lies at the heart of a final answer to the question 'Do Muslims and Christians worship the same god?' So in the final chapter we will turn to love and what God's love really means.

Key takeaways

- There is a difference between inheritance (where one idea grows naturally or organically out of another) and borrowing (where something is ripped from its context and used in a whole new setting). The Qur'an has borrowed heavily from Jewish and Christian thought, with many stories and characters losing much of their meaning as they were inserted into qur'anic theology. What has happened to Jesus in the Qur'an is the example par excellence of this process.

- Jesus is discussed in some ninety verses of the Qur'an (and mentioned by name in twenty-five of those), but he doesn't fit into Islam. His virgin birth, his impressive collection of miracles, the lofty titles the Qur'an uses for him and his dramatic return and actions at the end of history – all these make him stand out from every other qur'anic prophet. Jesus simply refuses to fit the mould into which Islam tries to squeeze him.

- But Jesus *does* fit into Christianity and into the Bible, where it is abundantly clear that he is far more than just-another-prophet. This is made clear by the fact that, on almost every page of the New Testament, Jesus is depicted as receiving worship (and in Judaism, worship was due to Yahweh and Yahweh alone).

- The early Christians worshipped Jesus because of the exalted claims he made about himself – putting his actions, teaching and even his name on a par with those of Yahweh. Jesus was eventually crucified for these claims, but his resurrection from the dead dramatically vindicated everything he had said about himself.

- The Bible is clear: if you want to know what Yahweh is really like (a God who is relational, knowable, loving and who has suffered on our behalf), then take a look at Jesus, who is God-with-us.

9

For the love of God, come home

Why Christianity is the most inclusive exclusive faith in the world

I have long enjoyed collecting the stories of lesser-known and unusual heroes, men and women whose endeavours set them apart in some way from the rest of us. Among the myriad biographies I have lining my shelves, the person who, for me, stands out from them all is Maximilian Kolbe.[1]

Born in Poland in 1894 into a devout Catholic family, Maximilian grew up to become a Franciscan friar, devoting his life to teaching, writing and missionary work. When Poland fell to the Nazis at the start of the Second World War, Maximilian began first passively and then more actively resisting the Nazi regime – publishing articles against the occupiers and helping to shelter Jews in his monastery at Niepokalanów. Finally the Nazis grew tired of the troublesome friar and on 17 February 1941 Maximilian was arrested by the Gestapo and thrown into the notorious Auschwitz concentration camp, where his name was stripped from him and he was known merely as prisoner number 16670.

Three months later, a prisoner escaped from Auschwitz, and when this was discovered at the evening roll call, the authorities were furious. Determined to deter future escape attempts, the deputy camp commandant, Karl Fritzsch, announced that he would choose ten men at random; they would then be locked up in an underground

---

1 There are several biographies of Maximilian Kolbe; in what follows, I am broadly following Elaine Murray Stone, *Maximilian Kolbe: Saint of Auschwitz* (New York: Paulist Press, 1997), especially pp. 71–91.

bunker and left to starve to death. This would send a message: if you escape from Auschwitz, *this* is what we will do to your friends.

Guards began to pace up and down the lines of prisoners, pulling out men at random, and when one man, Franciszek Gajowniczek (who had been jailed for aiding the Polish Resistance) was chosen, he began sobbing hysterically. 'Please,' Gajowniczek wept. 'Have pity! I have a wife and two children! Whatever will become of them?'

On hearing Gajowniczek's cries, Maximilian stepped out of the crowd of prisoners and addressed the commandant: 'May I make a request?' Nobody had ever dared speak to the commandant like that before and, taken aback, Karl Fritzsch barked at him: 'What do you want?' Maximilian pointed at the sobbing Gajowniczek and calmly replied, 'I wish to take the place of this man.'

The commandant stared in sheer disbelief at Maximilian before finally replying, 'I grant your request.' At those words, Gajowniczek was released back into the crowd of prisoners while Maximilian was dragged away with the other nine condemned men and herded into a death cell in the basement of Auschwitz Building 13, where the group were locked up in the dark, without food or water. Over the next few days, Maximilian led the prisoners in hymn singing and prayer, as one by one each succumbed to his fate. Finally, two weeks later, only Maximilian was left alive and, needing the cell for other victims, the Nazis executed him by lethal injection.

How do we know the details of Maximilian's story? Because Franciszek Gajowniczek was freed four years later when Auschwitz was liberated by the Russian army; he spent the rest of his life spreading the story of Maximilian's incredible act of sacrifice. On one occasion, asked how he felt about what Maximilian had done, Gajowniczek replied, 'The immensity of Friar Kolbe's death regularly overwhelms me. I, the condemned, lived because someone willingly offered his own life for me.'

Why did Maximilian do this? What drove him to offer his life, self-sacrificially, for another? The answer is that as a deeply committed

Christian, Maximilian was doing his best to live out the words of Jesus, who said, 'Greater love has no one than this: to lay down one's life for one's friends' (John 15:13).

Love is not cheap

'Love' is a word that is heard a lot these days. It's a word thrown around all too casually in our culture, so much so that it is in danger of losing its meaning entirely. We talk about loving our jobs and smartphones, our pets and our hobbies, our houses and cars, even – for those who don't have the misfortune to follow Neasden Football Club[2] – loving our sports teams. Even when the word 'love' is applied to human relationships, it can all too often be used casually or even cynically. Maybe some of you reading this have heard someone declare, 'I love you', only then to be let down badly by that person.

Thus when somebody says, 'I think god is love', as so many people instinctively believe god must be, it's important to ask, 'What do you mean by "love"?' After all, if love is just a synonym for 'like', or a feeling, or a 'second-hand emotion' (to quote Tina Turner), or just a warm gooey feeling we get when staring into another person's eyes over dinner at the local Italian trattoria,[3] then what does it mean to say that 'god is love'?

This is why Jesus' words, defining the greatest, the highest, the purest form of love as self-sacrifice, are so powerful and so helpful. They give us a standard, a model, of what real love looks like: namely

---

2 Neasden FC have been led to defeat after defeat in the North Circular Relegation League by ashen-faced manager Ron Knee (59). Their sorry history is recorded in Sid and Doris Bonkers, *Neasden FC: The only way is up* (Privata Oculo Press, 2013).

3 The idea of Italian restaurants and romance are forever marred for me because in my first year of marriage, I took my wife for dinner at a lovely little pizzeria near where we lived. Leaning in for a kiss at the end of the meal, I got too close to a candle and set my hair alight. 'You're on fire!' shrieked Astrid, which I initially took to be a compliment about my rugged charm and general irresistibility, until she followed up by tipping a glass of water over my head.

the willingness to so put other people first, you would be willing to lay down your life for them.

I find it fascinating that everybody instinctively knows that Jesus was right. From the most pious religious person (of whatever faith) to the most dogmatic secularist, we all know, deep down, that there is something very special going on when one person gives his or her life for another. Whether it's in literature, such as Charles Dickens' story *A Tale of Two Cities*, where Sydney Carton bravely substitutes himself for Charles Darnay and is killed in his place so that Charles can go free. Or in a news report, where we hear of a mother giving her life for her child. Or in the military, when we read the account of somebody like Billy McFadzean, the twenty-year-old soldier who, during the Battle of the Somme in the First World War, threw himself on top of some live grenades that had fallen into a trench. They exploded, killing Billy, but his rapid action saved the lives of dozens of his comrades – an action for which he was posthumously awarded the Victoria Cross.[4] Or the story of Maximilian Kolbe, who was willing to be condemned to death in the place of another. Accounts like these move us deeply, because we know in the very fibre of our being that self-sacrificial love is incredibly impressive. Real love is not cheap, true love is costly, and the highest form of love is self-sacrifice – love that is willing to expend itself for another, even at the price of one's own life.

So how does that help us begin to tease out what we mean when we say 'god is love'? Well, think about the famous cry of devout Muslims: '*Allahu akbar*' ('God is greater!'). My Muslim friends are absolutely right: God is great, but I also think they are being too modest and we can say more: God is not merely *greater* – he is the *very greatest*. And thus, by definition, anything that God does must be the greatest example: God is the greatest creator, the greatest judge, the greatest ruler, and so on. Which means that *if* God is a god

---

4 See 'William McFadzean VC', *Royal Irish Virtual Military Gallery*, <www.royal-irish.com/persons/william-mcfadzean-vc>.

of love, then the love that he displays must be the greatest, the highest form of love that there is. And as we instinctively know (and as Jesus clearly explained), that means self-sacrificial, costly love. Only if God has demonstrated self-sacrificial love can he truly be said to be loving. Anything else is just words, and when it comes to love, we need more than words.

Compassion means more than moralizing

Something very similar is going on when we look at a word that is closely related to 'love', namely 'compassion'. As we saw in chapter 4, the Qur'an is somewhat reticent to describe Allah as loving, tiptoeing around the term like somebody creeping barefoot and blindfolded through a room full of mousetraps. But for all of its nervousness about love, the Qur'an is very happy to describe Allah as compassionate. For example, the very first verse of the Qur'an announces: 'In the Name of [Allah], the Merciful, the Compassionate' (Q. 1:1).

That little sentence is known in Islam as the *bismillah*, and when Muslims recite the Qur'an, it is recited before each chapter (with the exception of the ninth), while the formulaic phrase 'Allah is forgiving and compassionate' is found in the Qur'an some forty-seven times. The Qur'an is thus insistent that Allah is a God who is compassionate.

The same is true when it comes to the Bible, which is also clear that Yahweh is a God of compassion. The Bible often pairs the word 'compassion' with 'love', stating things like:

Yahweh is compassionate and gracious,
slow to anger and abundant in loyal love.
(Psalm 103:8 LEB)

But, as with the word 'love', we need to ask what the word 'compassion' means. How, for example, does it differ from words like 'empathy', or 'kindness', or terms like 'not-bouncing-my-son-upside-down-by-the-ankles-when-he-has-left-his-room-in-a-mess-for-the-seventh-day-running'?[5]

According to the Oxford English Dictionary, the word 'compassion' is what linguists call a compound word – a word that was made by gluing two other words together. In the case of 'compassion', it was formed originally by sticking together two Latin words: *com*, meaning 'with', and *pati*, meaning 'to suffer'. The word 'compassion' literally means 'to suffer alongside'.

Although these roots of the word 'compassion' are centuries old, we still instinctively understand them if you think about how we use the word. For example, imagine you are walking down the street when you see a person being racially abused. You shout out to the other passers-by, 'Racism is wrong!' And then, for good measure, you pull out your smartphone and tweet hashtags like #RacismIsAwful a few times, along with a concerned emoticon or two.

Or imagine that on your walk home from work, you pass a homeless person, sleeping rough in a shop doorway. Stunned by such a scene of deprivation in a modern city, you cry out to your fellow pedestrians, 'Poverty is wrong!' And then you rush on home and buy a T-shirt with some anti-poverty slogans on it from Amazon.[6]

In either case, you have not been compassionate. Yes, you have been angered by the injustice and poverty. You may have even wept tears as you tweeted. But if all you did was shout and protest, then you haven't been compassionate. You have just moralized (and worse, virtue-signalled). Calling out injustice without actually doing anything is not compassion.

---

5 The Germans are *bound* to have a single multisyllabic word for just this very thing. This is a nation, don't forget, that coined the forty-one-letter extravaganza *Donaudampfschiffahrtsgesellschaftskapitän* to denote 'Danube steamship company captain'. I am pained by the fact that English has no equivalent, as this is a word I am sure I could use on a daily basis.

6 Because, of course, the best way to tackle poverty is to send money to large corporations.

But now, rerun the thought experiments. Next time you see a person being racially abused, you rush across the street to defend him or her from the bullies, even though they are bigger and more numerous than you. Maybe you even get beaten up yourself as you try to defend the victim. But that's true compassion: you did something, it cost you, and you suffered alongside. Or next time you see a homeless person sleeping rough, you actually stop to help; maybe you buy him or her a meal or even offer a bed for the night. Now *that's* compassion, because you got involved and it cost you personally.

Compassion means more than just moralizing. More than just pointing out that something is wrong. More than just judging the situation. Compassion means getting involved, sometimes at great cost, possibly even with a risk to yourself, and maybe even if it causes suffering to you personally.

So what, then, does it mean to speak of god as 'compassionate'? Unless we are simply playing word games, then it is only meaningful to call god compassionate if the god we are talking about hasn't merely told us what he *thinks* about injustice and suffering, poverty and pain, but has also done something – and done something which has cost him, an action through which he has suffered alongside us.

When we look at the Qur'an, it is clear that Allah has *not* acted in this way. For sure, the Qur'an tells us what Allah *thinks* about injustice and our part in it. What he thinks is that it is wrong and that human beings need to wise up, or judgment will follow. But Allah has *done* nothing about our predicament: he has not become involved, nor has he has suffered with us to tackle the problem. In short, Allah is a moralizer, but he is not compassionate.

By contrast, Yahweh is very different. The Bible tells us time and again not simply that Yahweh disapproves of and is angry at injustice and suffering, but that Yahweh cares so deeply for his people that he is *moved* to action, stepping into history in the person of Jesus in order to do something about suffering and evil, demonstrating far more than words but showing true compassion – suffering alongside us and displaying, in the equivalent of letters written miles high across the sky, how great his love is for us. As the Bible unpacks what Yahweh's compassion and love in action look like, it holds nothing back:

> For I am convinced that neither death nor life, neither angels nor demons, neither the present nor the future, nor any powers, neither height nor depth, nor anything else in all creation, will be able to separate us from the love of God that is in Christ Jesus our Lord.
> (Romans 8:38–39)

Think about who Jesus claimed to be: God come in the flesh, stepping into space and time, God getting his feet dirty with the dust of the world, and his hands bloody with the nails of the world. If that claim of Jesus stands up, then what we see in his willingness to go to the cross to deal with our brokenness, sinfulness and shame is not just the greatest act of self-sacrificial love by the greatest being who exists, but a powerful, beautiful and practical demonstration of what compassion really looks like. In Jesus, we see displayed a God who loved us so much that even while we were his enemies, he was willing to do all that for us.

In his autobiography, former Muslim Nabeel Qureshi describes the love of Yahweh that was so attractive to him as he came to the end of his four-year journey from Islam to Christianity:

> The good news is that God Himself loves us enough to enter into the world and suffer for us, that despite humanity's inability to save itself, God saved us. He did not send someone else to do His dirty work. He rescued us Himself. No one else could do it. That is the beauty of the gospel; it is all about God and what He has done out of His love for us.[7]

---

7 Nabeel Qureshi, *Seeking Allah, Finding Jesus: A devout Muslim encounters Christianity*, 3rd edn (Grand Rapids, MI: Zondervan, 2018), p. 288.

The attraction of Jesus

The attractiveness of Jesus that first intrigued Nabeel Qureshi is something that many people have been drawn to, whether they are Christians, Muslims, seekers or sceptics. It is no accident that leading atheists sometimes speak movingly of Jesus' character, or why in the centuries after Muhammad, thousands of stories and traditions about Jesus circulated in early Islam,[8] and why the Qur'an itself tries to co-opt Jesus. People see in him something unique, attractive and compelling, even if they don't know quite what to do with him after they have borrowed him.

Some years ago I was speaking at an interfaith panel at the Canadian Parliament in Ottawa. After the event there was a reception, and as I grazed the pluralistic buffet – wholesome foodstuffs like non-alcoholic cheese, vegan wine and meat-based vegetable substitutes – I was introduced to a distinguished-looking woman who was a senior leader of the Baha'i community. If you are unfamiliar with the Baha'i, they are members of a newer religious movement, founded by the Persian mystic Baha'u'llah in 1863. They are also classic pluralists and have co-opted everyone from Buddha to Muhammad to Jesus into their attempt to teach the essential oneness of all religions.

As we chatted, the woman asked about my PhD and I explained how I had used computer analysis to study how the Qur'an was first composed and put together. She began to look very nervous and eventually asked, 'So does all this evidence lead you to conclude that Muhammad wasn't a prophet?'

I politely replied that this was something of an understatement and that this is the kind of problem you have if, like the Baha'i, you grab hold of every religious idea you can lay hands on without under-standing it, like a starving student in an all-you-can-gobble-for-a-pound fast-food joint. 'Besides,' I added, 'my other concern is how

---

8   See the extensive collection in Tarif Khalidi, *The Muslim Jesus: Sayings and stories in Islamic literature* (Cambridge, MA: Harvard University Press, 2001), pp. 47–220.

the Baha'i faith has tried to shoehorn Jesus into the just-another-prophet box, failing to understand that Jesus never saw himself as one option among many, but as uniquely the way to encounter God.'

The woman almost choked on her gluten-and-dairy-free, low-fat scone and spluttered, 'What . . . what . . . what *on earth* gives you the impression that Jesus thought anything even remotely like that?'

'Oh, I don't know, perhaps something like chapter fourteen, verse six, of the Gospel of John, where Jesus famously said, "I am the way, the truth and the life. Nobody comes to God the Father except through me."'

There was a brief silence, as she chewed in that determined way that gluten-free-flour products always require in order to be swallow-able, before she replied, 'Do you know, that verse has always given me considerable trouble.'

She is not alone. Lots of people have trouble with John 14:6 and Jesus' claim not merely to be *a* way to God, or to be teaching *some* truth, or to have some thoughts about life, the universe, and so forth, but rather to be *the* way, *the* truth and *the* life. Once again, we're forced to make a choice here: either Jesus was breathtakingly arrogant, making even the most self-obsessed celebrity look like a paragon of humility, or else he could say this kind of stuff calmly and rationally because it was true.

But of course the real reason why many people baulk at 'I am the way, the truth and the life' is because it looks terribly exclusivist. If Jesus is all those things, what about those who think differently, or who are followers of other faiths? Isn't this terribly narrow?

Not really.

It *would* be incredibly narrow if Jesus was saying and Christians were repeating words to the effect of 'Jesus is the only way to God; Christians are therefore better than anybody else because they've worked it out and are going to heaven; and the rest of you are a bunch of unlucky fools for not following him.' It would also be equally narrow if Jesus was suggesting that only the very best, the very smartest, cleverest or holiest, could qualify to follow him. 'Those of you who make the grade, come on in! The rest of you – there's the exit, and please don't leave any sticky fingerprints on your way out.'

But neither of those things is what Jesus is saying.

Rather, what Jesus is offering is an *open* exclusivism. Yes, he is the only way – the only way to really see, in action far more than words, God's love and compassion, mercy and forgiveness, generosity and kindness. The only way by which our sinfulness and brokenness can be dealt with and the only way by which we are able to call God 'Father'. But that way is open to *anybody*: no matter what your background, race, gender, age or religious heritage – and certainly no matter if your life up to this point hasn't exactly measured up and you're dragging more baggage with you than an airport luggage carousel.

Jesus may be the only way, but he is a way open to all who are eager to seek, desperate to find, and prepared to lay down their lives and follow. As Jesus said:

So I say to you: ask and it will be given to you; seek and you will find; knock and the door will be opened to you. For everyone who asks receives; the one who seeks finds; and to the one who knocks, the door will be opened.
(Luke 11:9–10)

Getting the question right

The question that we have been exploring throughout this book, 'Do Muslims and Christians worship the same god?', is an important one and, as we have seen, a doorway into a wide range of connected issues. But despite its helpfulness, it does have some flaws, perhaps the biggest of which is that it tries to do too much. Let me illustrate what I mean. My five-year-old son, Christopher, loves playing Twenty Questions, one of those old parlour games invented back in the days when people hadn't discovered television, narcissistic social media usage or other ways to avoid actually talking to one another.

The game begins with one person, the answerer, thinking of an object and the other players trying to guess it by asking questions to which the answerer can only reply 'Yes' or 'No'. The one exception is the first question asked, which traditionally is not 'Is there something more exciting we can play?' but 'Animal, vegetable or mineral?' My son has this first question mastered – but then, on hearing the answer 'Animal', has a tendency to leap straight to the taxonomically hyper-specific like 'Is it a lesser striped African swallow?'

The problem here, as I regularly point out to my son, is that this is making the question 'Animal, vegetable or mineral?' do too much work. There is a host of other questions we need to ask before we can decide whether the animal in question is an African (or European) swallow, mutant rabbit or some other fantastic beast.

If we are not careful, something similar occurs when we ask, 'Do Muslims and Christians worship the same god?' There are actually two different questions wrapped up in that larger question and it may be helpful to tease them apart. The first is the question of whether the Qur'an describes and teaches about the same god as the God of the Bible. In short, are Allah and Yahweh the same person? As I have argued over the course of this book, the answer is a categorical 'No'. When we look at the key characteristics of Yahweh in the Bible (relational, knowable, holy, loving, and having suffered), these are all missing or denied in the Qur'an. Furthermore, when we explore what Yahweh and Allah have to say about who human beings are, what has gone wrong in the world and what the solution to that wrongness is, Yahweh and Allah have fundamentally different answers to each question.

The conclusion is unavoidable: Allah and Yahweh, as described by the Qur'an and the Bible, are utterly, irreconcilably different. To try to argue otherwise – even for the very best of motives, such as wanting to encourage religious harmony – leads to utterly misreading, mishandling and mangling the texts of the Bible and the Qur'an. If you have to pound a jigsaw piece with a sledgehammer to make it fit, you probably have the wrong piece, in the wrong place, or even entirely the wrong jigsaw.

But there's another question lurking inside 'Do Muslims and Christians worship the same god?', namely the question of whether *some* Muslims are yearning for and seeking after Yahweh, the God of the Bible, even without realizing it. I think the answer here is 'Yes'.

In the New Testament, in the book of Acts, which describes the growth of the early church in the decades after the resurrection of Jesus, there is a fascinating episode in chapter 17. Paul, a former persecutor of the early church who had become a Christian after a dramatic encounter with the risen Jesus, is on a missionary journey in Athens, one of the key cultural centres of the ancient world. As he walks around, Paul notices all the idols and temples that adorn the city and, as a good monotheistic Jew, becomes quite upset. But then he notices something: the Athenians have an altar inscribed 'To an unknown god'. In order to cover their bases, in case in all their temple building the Athenians had accidentally overlooked Kevin the God of Lost Socks or something, they had built an altar marked with the first-century equivalent of 'To whom it may concern'.

When he sees this, Paul doesn't reject it as yet another example of the Athenians' misguided religiosity, but sees it as a place to start from in his conversations with them. So when invited to address the philosophers and thinkers who met at the Areopagus, a rocky outcrop near the Acropolis, Paul launches into his speech by saying:

People of Athens! I see that in every way you are very religious. For as I walked around and looked carefully at your objects of worship, I even found an altar with this inscription: TO AN UNKNOWN GOD. So you are ignorant of the very thing you worship – and this is what I am going to proclaim to you. (Acts 17:22–23)

From there, Paul goes on to explain how the real God doesn't live in temples, but is the one who made everything. (He even quotes the Athenians' own poets at them as he builds his presentation.) Finally, he connects all this to how that God stepped into history in the person of Jesus Christ, demonstrating this through his resurrection. On hearing all this, some laugh at Paul, but others become followers of Jesus.

Throughout Acts chapter 17, the Bible makes it clear that some people are reaching out towards the God of the Bible even though they don't know it. And I think that some Muslims are in that position. I often meet Muslims who tell me they believe that God is love, even though the Qur'an makes no such claim. Often in those conversations I have found it helpful to say something along the lines of 'Yes! Yes, God *is* a god of love. Let me tell you more about him, because the god you are drawn to sounds like the God of the Bible.'

Some of the Athenians were nearer than they realized to Yahweh: they had figured out there was another god they hadn't yet discovered; they just hadn't put the whole jigsaw together. And for Muslims who are drawn to the idea of a god of love, who are looking for a god who is more than just commands-and-laws-and-prescriptions-and-sharia, but a god who has demonstrated and displayed the love that he has for us, a god who invites us to call him 'Father', to them I want to say: *Come on home!*

When Nabeel Qureshi responded to that offer and powerfully encountered the love of Yahweh in and through Jesus, his life was turned upside down: 'Over the next few days, my heart was filled with a new joy, the joy of meeting God Himself. I thought I had known Him my entire life, but now that I knew who He really was, there was no comparison. Nothing compares to the one true God.'[9]

Jesus invites all of us to come on home to the love of God. But responding to that invitation is not always easy. For some of us there may be family or cultural pressures to believe something different;

---

9 Qureshi, *Seeking Allah, Finding Jesus*, p. 277.

it can take real courage to consider the invitation of Jesus. For others, pride or self-reliance may hold us back. It is tough to admit that we have been wrong, and it can be hard to acknowledge that we can't make our lives measure up through our own grit and determination but that we need God's help and rescue. But don't miss out on God's love, forgiveness and welcome because of fear, pride, or a foolish desire to show everybody how clever, moral and 'religious' you are. The door to God's house is wide open. Don't miss the invitation because you insist on ignoring the open doorway, declaring that you will instead attempt to rock-climb three storeys up the sheer back wall and then abseil your way down the chimney, all by your own efforts.

Forgiveness is free (but very costly)

Jesus told a famous story to illustrate the tendency we have as humans to miss the love and welcome that God offers to us.[10] He began by telling how there was once a man who had two sons, the younger of whom clearly had an attitude problem that makes modern teenagers look positively angelic by comparison:

> The younger one said to his father, 'Father, give me my share of the estate.' So [the father] divided his property between [his two sons].
> (Luke 15:12)

The younger son's request is shocking. In asking for his inheritance now, he's wishing his father dead. He is effectively saying, 'Dad, I'm tired of sitting around waiting for you to die; you look far too healthy

---

10 Luke 15:11–32. In what follows, I am drawing heavily on the work of Ken Bailey, whose studies of how Jesus' stories were understood in the Middle East have become classics. See Kenneth E. Bailey, *The Cross and the Prodigal: Luke 15 through the eyes of Middle Eastern peasants*, 2nd edn (Downers Grove, IL: IVP, 2005); and Kenneth E. Bailey, *Jesus through Middle Eastern Eyes: Cultural studies in the Gospels* (London: SPCK, 2008). The story is also unpacked in a very contemporary way by Timothy Keller, *The Prodigal God: Recovering the heart of the Christian faith* (London: Hodder & Stoughton, 2009).

and I've got plans, so could we proceed as if you were dead, and you give me my inheritance now?'

Rather than disciplining his errant offspring, the father does something very surprising: he complies with the request, sharing his money not just with his younger son but also with the elder son, as he divides his money *between them*. In the Middle East of Jesus' day, the elder son would have received two thirds, the younger son one third, so notice how we don't at this point hear the elder son pipe up, 'No, Dad! Please keep your money – let me talk some sense into this crazy brother of mine.' No, they both take the money, and then, as news and gossip spread fast in small Middle Eastern villages, the younger son runs away, liquidating his assets in a fire sale and hightailing it out of town:

> Not long after that, the younger son got together all he had, set off for a distant country and there squandered his wealth in wild living.
> (v. 13)

It is important to note that 'wild living' does not imply immorality; it simply means that the younger son lived well. As a typical Middle Easterner, he probably spent much of his money acquiring a reputation: throwing feasts, giving gifts, gaining friends and influence. Perhaps a few nice things for himself too: new clothes; a faster camel with chrome trimming, a V8 engine and a tilt-and-slide sunroof. But money never lasts for ever:

> After he had spent everything, there was a severe famine in that whole country, and he began to be in need.
> (v. 14)

Famines in the ancient world were a terrifying prospect. In the Western world, we are used to readily available food – a burger,

171

kebab or other takeaway on every corner. If things do go wrong, we have government support, welfare, charities, a safety net. But in the ancient world, famines simply spelt doom with a capital 'D'. If you had no resources, you died:

> So he went and hired himself out to a citizen of that country, who sent him to his fields to feed pigs. He longed to fill his stomach with the pods that the pigs were eating, but no one gave him anything.
> (vv. 15–16)

In a famine, work will be scarce and the young man has to hunt hard for a job, probably nagging and pestering people to hire him. I suspect the final citizen he approaches is suspicious of this peculiar-looking foreigner and so offers him a job he thinks a Jew won't take. (The problem with pigs, of course, is not just that they are dirty; pigs are also religiously unclean.) But the young man is desperate, so he takes it. He's now lost everything: alienated from his father and his family, far from home, poor, hungry and now religiously unclean. He thought he'd hit rock bottom, but has discovered there is a whole basement level beneath that to sink into too. So he hatches a cunning plan:

> When he came to his senses, he said, 'How many of my father's hired servants have food to spare, and here I am starving to death! I will set out and go back to my father and say to him: Father, I have sinned against heaven and against you. I am no longer worthy to be called your son; make me like one of your hired servants.' So he got up and went to his father.
> (vv. 17–20)

Notice how this has very little to do with repentance. The clue is what he *doesn't* say: no mention of shaming his family or of wishing his father dead. No apology at all for burning through a third of the family money. Rather, his whole carefully crafted little speech is about getting a meal and a job.[11] He wants to be taken back as a hired hand and paid a wage. Why? So he can pay his father back. He is thinking: if I can just earn some money (after having had a shower), I can eventually pay my father back and earn my way into his favour and forgiveness.

> So he got up and went to his father.
> (v. 20a)

We now come to one of the most shocking parts of the story:

> But while he was still a long way off, his father saw him and was filled with compassion for him; he ran to his son . . .'
> (v. 20b)

In the Middle East of Jesus' day, *fathers do not run*. Running is a young man's game. The head of the family, the patriarch, sits under a nice shady tree and directs other people while *they* run. The father probably hasn't run for decades. Furthermore, in order to run, he will need to lift up the front of his robes, exposing his legs, something incredibly shameful in the culture. In order to forgive and reconcile with his younger son, the son who dishonoured him, the father is willing to dishonour and shame himself. This is so shocking, so surprising, that in many parts of the Middle East this story is known as 'The Story of the Running Father'.

The father reached his son and:

> threw his arms round him and kissed him.
> (v. 20c)

---

11 It has been pointed out that the younger son here is basically quoting the words of Pharaoh from Exodus 10:16 where the Egyptian king pretends to repent in an attempt to manipulate Moses into doing what he wants. See Kenneth E. Bailey, *Jacob and the Prodigal: How Jesus retold Israel's story* (Downers Grove, IL: IVP, 2003), p. 106.

There is, it must be said, a *lot* of kissing in the Middle East. I remember doing a speaking tour through the region a few years ago and regularly being enthusiastically embraced by large, bearded men who would kiss me on both cheeks. As a Brit whose idea of personal space extends to about a mile out, I am still in therapy. But in the Middle East of Jesus' day, kissing was very symbolic. Servants would kiss their master's feet; students would kiss their teacher's hand; friends and family would kiss on the face – a sign of peace and welcome.

But fighting himself free from his father's embrace, the younger son, who has spent a lot of time rehearsing his clever little speech and isn't about to let it go to waste, puts on his best I-am-a-very-sorry-and-humble-son face, aims for a BAFTA and launches in:

> The son said to him, 'Father, I have sinned against heaven and against you. I am no longer worthy to be called your son.'
> (v. 21)

I imagine that the son gets about halfway through his speech before realizing that this is not about economics and earning his way in, but about *forgiveness*. And forgiveness is always a gift and is always free:

> But the father said to his servants, 'Quick! Bring the best robe and put it on him. Put a ring on his finger and sandals on his feet.'
> (v. 22)

Each gift mentioned here is costly: the robe is probably one of the father's best. People will see the son wearing it and know what it means – the son is back in the family. The sandals are also symbolic: servants go barefoot, but sons wear shoes. All of this has cost the father financially, but the greatest price he has paid has been his honour. The father has borne the dishonour and humiliation that has been heaped on him, out of his self-sacrificial love for his son. So now the father instructs his servants:

'Bring the fattened calf and kill it. Let's have a feast and celebrate. For this son of mine was dead and is alive again; he was lost and is found.' And so they began to celebrate.
(vv. 23–24)

Not everybody was happy about the return of the younger son, and by far the unhappiest was the fatted calf. Out there in the field, munching on grain, thinking how wonderful life is. Then words like 'feast' drift across from the house along with the sounds and smells of a barbecue being lit. It's too late for aerobics and a weight-loss programme now.

A fatted calf is a *big* piece of meat. This is no mere family meal the father has planned, but a feast to which the entire village will be invited. The son has been welcomed back into the family; now it's time to bring him back into the community, among whom he would have been a laughing stock and an outcast.

But now we meet the elder son again:

Meanwhile, the elder son was in the field. When he came near the house, he heard music and dancing. So he called one of the servants and asked him what was going on. 'Your brother has come,' he replied, 'and your father has killed the fattened calf because he has him back safe and sound.'
(vv. 25–27)

On hearing what has just happened, the elder son's blood boils and the red mist descends. If his stupid younger brother has been welcomed back, received with peace and forgiveness, it's too late to rush into the house and yell, 'Make the idiotic fool get a job!' So now it's the elder son's turn to humiliate and dishonour his father:

> The elder brother became angry and refused to go in. So his
> father went out and pleaded with him.
> (v. 28).

For the second time this day, the father has to go out and meet a son,
but this time the elder, allegedly more responsible one, who is outside
sulking and ranting. Bad enough at the best of times, but the whole
village is here, and Number One Son is making a scene and embar-
rassing and shaming the entire family. The elder son lets rip with
both barrels:

> He answered his father, 'Look! All these years I've been slaving
> for you and never disobeyed your orders. Yet you never gave
> me even a young goat so I could celebrate with my friends. But
> when this son of yours who has squandered your property
> with prostitutes comes home, you kill the fattened calf for
> him!'
> (vv. 29–30)

Look at the insults: the elder son doesn't say 'Beloved Dad' or
'Respected Father'. Rather, he just says 'Look!' – the equivalent of
'Oi, you, old guy!' He can't even call the younger son 'my brother' –
it's 'this son of yours'. And his character is coming out too: he's as
money-obsessed as his brother. 'You've given me nothing!' he
screams, spittle flying. But wait: *nothing*? In verse 12 he was given
two thirds of the entire family estate. He's so angry he's making
things up.

But notice something else about his complaint. Who does he want
to party with? Not his family. He wants to party with his friends; he
wants to be his own man, just like his younger brother. Perhaps
he even secretly envies his younger brother's rebellion and wishes he
had the courage to do the same. But as his rants die away, the father
now speaks up:

'My son,' the father said, 'you are always with me, and everything I have is yours. But we had to celebrate and be glad, because this brother of yours was dead and is alive again; he was lost and is found.'

(vv. 31–32)

And there Jesus ends the story, with the father's words of invitation hanging in the air, the doorway to the house open and the party beginning. I suspect Jesus left the ending open because he wanted the first hearers – and he wants us – to think about how *we* will respond.

The story is fascinating because the two sons each made the same mistake: both thought their job was to earn their way into their father's affections. The younger son messed up badly but then thought: let's buy my way back in. The elder son, legalistic and law-keeping to a fault, thought to himself: if you don't obey and measure up, you aren't welcome. It's deeply ironic that at the end of the story, the freely forgiven sinner ends up in his father's family; the religious keeper-of-the-last-dot-of-the-law ends up outside.

With the very greatest respect, I think that Islam encourages both of the tendencies seen in the two sons in Jesus' story. On the one hand, the 'solution' that Allah in the Qur'an offers to our sin and rebellion is: work hard, pay me back, keep your nose clean and earn your way in. That's the younger brother's approach to his father in Jesus' story. Equally, Islam can also encourage a response not unlike the elder brother's: look at all the commands I've kept. More than once I have had conversations with Muslim friends who are almost offended at the idea that through Jesus, God might just forgive people before they have sorted out the sorry mess of their lives: how can God just forgive a person like that? That's exactly the protest of the elder son in Jesus' story.

But forgiveness, by its very nature, is free to the one who receives it and costly to the giver, just as the father in the story paid not just in money but also in reputation and honour, or just as the forgiveness that the God of the Bible offers us is not free, but cost Jesus his life.

The good news of the Bible, the wonderful news of what God has done in Jesus, is that the door to God's household is flung wide open. The lights are on and the party has begun – and there is room at the table for everyone. More than that, there's a huge welcome into God's loving family. Yes, the only way into God's house is *through* Jesus, but that way is open to all who are willing to lay down their pride and self-reliance.

The road that leads to home

A year or so ago, I was invited to take part in a question-and-answer evening at a leading Scottish university. A friend and I sat on the stage in front of almost 200 students, of all faiths and none, and answered questions about Christianity for almost two hours. And the students asked about *everything*: from science to suffering, religious wars to discrimination – the list went on. But time and time again, the questions kept circling back to Jesus: who was he? What was he all about? What's the evidence for his life and teaching?

At the end of the evening, a student came up to speak to us. He introduced himself as a Muslim and said that for over a year now, he had been carefully investigating the claims of Jesus – as well as putting the claims of Islam, the faith of his upbringing, to the test. Quietly he said to us, 'I am increasingly of the view that everything Jesus said about himself is true. But following him will be very costly – my family, my community, my . . .' and his voice trailed away. Finally he spoke up again: 'Would you . . . would you pray with me? Would you pray that I might have the courage to look clearly at Jesus, to pursue the trail of evidence where it leads, and perhaps – perhaps even to follow Jesus one day?'

As we had the honour of praying with that brave young man, I was incredibly moved. Moved that he had so clearly seen something deeply attractive and compelling about Jesus; encouraged that he had committed to properly looking into who Jesus was; and impressed that he had worked out there were choices to be made and had realized it would take courage as well as integrity to make them.

And that is my prayer for all of you who have read this far, especially for my Muslim readers. Thank you for sticking with the book, despite all the challenges and questions it may have raised in your minds. My prayer is that you would discover for yourself what it means that God is not distant but relational; that not just his commands but God *himself* can be known; that God does not merely approve of those who earn his favour, but is truly loving in his deepest nature; that God does not stand at a distance, shouting instructions that do not solve our deepest problems, but has acted in order to rescue us, suffering alongside as he did so.

Too many debates about faith revolve around questions like 'Does god exist?' or 'Which religion is true?' Those are not unimportant questions, but I believe they can distract us from the far more essential question 'Who is god and what is he truly like?' I fully and firmly believe that who God is can be seen most clearly in and through Jesus, whom the Bible describes as 'God with us'. There really is nobody like the God of the Bible, nobody like Jesus. And his offer of peace, forgiveness and welcome into his family is free for anyone who repents and believes: so *come on home*.

Key takeaways

- Jesus taught that the greatest form of love is self-sacrificial love, laying down one's life for another. If god is a loving god, the love he displays must be the greatest form of love (because everything god does is the greatest), so only if god has demonstrated self-sacrificial love can he truly be said to be loving.

- As well as describing god as 'loving', many religions also want to speak of god as 'compassionate'. But compassion means more than just words or moralizing: compassion requires action. If god is truly compassionate, he must have not merely *said* something about injustice, evil and suffering but also *done* something about it.

- For the Bible, if we want to see God's love and compassion in action, we should look at Jesus. Jesus said that if we want to truly know God's love and be able to call him 'Father', this is freely possible – but only through him.

- Jesus' claims like this were exclusivist, but what Jesus offers is not a narrow exclusivism but an open exclusivism – open to all who repent, trust and believe, no matter their background or the baggage they are carrying.

- Forgiveness by its very nature is costly to the one doing the forgiving, but free to the one who is being forgiven. Forgiveness that must be bought, earned or worked for is no forgiveness at all.

- If you believe that god is truly loving and genuinely compassionate, you are close to the God of the Bible. Why not take a look at Jesus and respond to his offer of forgiveness and welcome?

Further reading

If you would like to explore some of the themes, topics and ideas in *Do Muslims and Christians Worship the Same God?* further, you will find a helpful list of resources below. I have given each a rating in terms of difficulty: popular-level pieces have a one-chilli rating (); slightly deeper-level items are rated as two chillies (); and more scholarly resources are marked with three chillies (). You don't need to be a specialist to enjoy a resource, but you will need to be prepared to put a little more effort in to get the most out of it.

General resources

  Short Answers videos, <www.solas-cpc.org/category/video/shortanswers>. This is a series of short films that we've produced at Solas, the organization I lead. Each five-minute episode tackles a common objection to, or question about, the Christian faith. We release a new film every two weeks.

Personal stories of Muslims who discovered the uniqueness of Jesus

  Nabeel Qureshi, *Seeking Allah, Finding Jesus: A devout Muslim encounters Christianity*, 3rd edn (Grand Rapids, MI: Zondervan, 2018). The exciting story of Nabeel's journey from Islam to Jesus. Personal, powerful and deeply honest, it is an absolute page-turner of a book.

  Bilquis Sheikh, *I Dared To Call Him Father: The miraculous story of a Muslim woman's encounter with*

181

God (Grand Rapids, MI: Chosen Books, 2003 [1978]). A beautifully written account of how a prominent Muslim woman in Asia came to discover the God she could call 'Father' as he began speaking to her, at first in dreams. Bilquis's story has touched the lives of many people around the world.

Abdu Murray, *Grand Central Question: Answering the critical concerns of the major worldviews* (Downers Grove, IL: IVP, 2014). Abdu was a Lebanese Shiite Muslim until God brought a number of Christians across his path who took his questions seriously. The book also explores how Christianity answers the key questions at the heart of many worldviews, not least Islam.

The Qur'an

Keith E. Small, *Holy Books Have a History: Textual histories of the New Testament and the Qur'an* (Kansas City, MO: Avant, 2011). Many people are unaware of the textual history of the Qur'an, including how it was composed and transmitted. This book takes a very fair look at both the Qur'an and the Bible, and introduces readers to some of the cutting-edge new work now being done on textual variants and other issues in early Qur'an manuscripts.

Mark Durie, *The Qur'an and Its Biblical Reflexes: Investigations into the genesis of a religion* (Lanham, MD: Lexington Books, 2018). Mark is both a linguist and a qur'anic expert, and his groundbreaking book explores how the Qur'an drew heavily on the Bible and Christian and Jewish tradition, reshaping what it borrowed to fit Islamic theology. If you want to know (in incredible detail) why Islam is *not* a sister religion to Christianity and Judaism, this is the book for you.

Understanding Jesus better

🦆 Richard Shumack, *Jesus through Muslim Eyes* (London: SPCK, 2020). A well-researched and easy-to-read look at the Jesus of the Qur'an, drawing a contrast with the Jesus of the Gospels. A great place to start if you want to understand Jesus better.

🦆🦆 Kenneth E. Bailey, *The Cross and the Prodigal: Luke 15 through the eyes of Middle Eastern peasants*, 2nd edn (Downers Grove, IL: IVP, 2005). A wonderful look at Jesus' 'Parable of the Father with Two Sons' from a Middle Eastern perspective. There is much in Jesus' famous story that is easy to miss, and Kenneth, drawing on a lifetime's experience of sharing Jesus' stories with Middle Easterners and Muslims, helps us better discover what we can learn about God, his fatherhood and his forgiveness, through Jesus' story.

🦆🦆🦆 Robert Bowman and J. Ed Komoszewski, *Putting Jesus in His Place: The case for the deity of Christ* (Grand Rapids, MI: Kregel, 2007). Want to *really* know why Christians believe that Jesus is God? Then this is the book you need. It's packed with hundreds of pages of detailed biblical evidence, digging deeply into the question 'Who did Jesus think he was?'

Understanding God better

🦆🦆 Michael Reeves, *Delighting in the Trinity: An introduction to the Christian faith* (Downers Grove, IL: IVP

Academic, 2012). One of the most confusing topics for Muslims when they look at Christianity is the doctrine of the Trinity – the biblical teaching that God has one nature but three persons: Father, Son and Spirit. This very readable little book sets out why this is not some abstract piece of theology but matters profoundly, in particular showing that it only makes sense to say that god is loving if he is a god who is Trinity.

Acknowledgments

The tentative first steps towards this book began back in 2016. I was living in Toronto and received a phone call from an old friend, KJ, in Chicago, asking if I would travel down and give a public lecture on the question 'Do Muslims and Christians worship the same god?'

'What a strange topic! Will anybody come?' I asked, wondering if something more mainstream, like 'Blaise Pascal's use of the apostrophe', might prove more popular.

KJ went on to explain that a professor at Wheaton College, a Christian liberal arts college near Chicago, had just caused huge controversy by publishing a post on social media proclaiming that Christians and Muslims worship the same god. 'We might get as many as three hundred people!' he exclaimed excitedly.

Americans are not especially famous for understatement, but KJ *wildly* underestimated. We got almost 700 and the auditorium was full to bursting.

Since then, I have spoken on 'Do Muslims and Christians worship the same god?' at universities, conferences, seminars and churches across Canada, the USA and Europe, and it's the same phenomenon: people flock to the sessions and venues are often standing-room only.

Thus, when I began thinking what to write after *The Atheist Who Didn't Exist* (2015), it seemed obvious to take my Chicago talk and expand it into a book. Not least because the idea that Muslims, Christians and Jews are all members of the 'Abrahamic faiths' and worship the same god was spreading, meme-like, throughout public discourse and general confusion was everywhere. Even well-regarded scholars (although non-experts in Islam) were wading in on the affirmative side. The Volf was at the door and I felt that there was a need for a proper response.

Acknowledgments

Much of the book was written during the COVID-19 pandemic and subsequent lockdown, which made it harder to procrastinate and avoid actually writing (my normal motto is Douglas Adams' aphorism 'I love deadlines. I love the whooshing noise they make as they go by'). After I had put up every set of shelves my wife could possibly want, taught myself the flamenco guitar and macramé, and weeded the garden within an inch of its life, there was nothing left to do *but* write, and so the book quickly took shape.

When not avoiding writing, I am an avid mountain climber. We are blessed in Scotland (where I live) with some wonderful hills, such as the Cairngorms, but with lockdown in place, I was restricted to Backmuir Wood, the small bit of woodland up the road from our house. At first, swapping 113 square miles and thousands of feet of rock, loch and corrie for a quarter-square-mile of fairly nondescript beech and pine trees was boring, especially after walking it a few dozen times.

But then I noticed something.

I noticed that when you spend time – *lots of time* – in a small area of land, you begin to see things in much more detail than ever before. Rather than just walking past a 'tree' or a 'bird', I began to be able to identify species and distinguish a hornbeam from a rowan, a magpie from a jay. As the British naturalist J. A. Baker remarked in his book *The Peregrine*: 'The hardest thing of all to see is what is really there.'[1]

That's a great metaphor for *Do Muslims and Christians Worship the Same God?* If you blunder through theology without paying attention, merely casually observing that Christians and Muslims both speak of 'God', you can lazily assume things are the same. But if you stop and look – really look hard and dig into the Qur'an and the Bible – then you begin to notice the differences. It soon becomes apparent that confusing Allah with Yahweh is less like mixing up a

---

1 J. A. Baker, *The Peregrine* (London: William Collins, 2010 [1967]), p. 33.

buzzard and a kestrel and more like confusing a woodpigeon with a badger.

My hope is that this book will cause people to look (and listen) more carefully. In the pluralistic world in which we live, it is important that people of all faiths (and none) learn to take the time to understand what each *really* believes – and not to be afraid of our differences. When it comes to both Islam and Christianity, we risk bending both entirely out of shape if our goal is purely to hammer them into the same mould.

There are many (*many!*) people I must thank for their help in making this book happen. First, a big thank you to KJ Johnson for initially inviting me to Chicago in 2016 to tackle this topic. Next up, a shout-out to the many friends who encouraged me as I was writing it, especially: Nick Chatrath (for swapping daily writing targets and terrible jokes); Richard Shumack (for bouncing theological ideas around); Kristi Mair (for wonderfully affirmative comments and text message threads that led down theological rabbit holes); my old Canadian colleagues who first encouraged me to write (especially Nathan Betts, Rick Manafo and David Cottrill); and new Scottish colleagues who kept Solas going while I wrote (especially Alan Dunn, David Hartnett, Tim Allyn, Gareth Black and Gavin 'Netball Is a Dangerous Sport' Matthews).

Thanks also to the absent friends to whom this book is dedicated: Nabeel Qureshi, whose journey from Islam to Christianity touched so many people; Keith Small, whose amazing scholarship on textual issues in early Qur'an manuscripts inspired me and so many others;[2] and Jamie Roth, a dear friend of our family in Canada, who was one of the funniest and sharpest thinkers I've met. You are all sorely missed and I wish you'd lived to see this book.

A few thanks on the practical producing-a-book side of things: thanks to Mark Sweeney, my ever-patient literary agent, who never

---

2   See, for example, Keith E. Small, *Textual Criticism and Qur'ān Manuscripts* (Lanham, MD: Lexington Books, 2011).

took 'I'm too busy to write right now' for an answer and kept on nudging; and, at (or formerly at) IVP, Tony Collins and Caleb Woodbridge for all their work throughout the many stages of bringing *Do Muslims and Christians Worship the Same God?* finally into existence. Thanks are also due to Mollie Barker, copy editor extraordinaire, for her endless professionalism, patience and willingness to indulge long discussions about plural pronouns.

I must also thank my family, who so faithfully gave me space and time to write – not easy during a COVID-19 lockdown, when we were all under one roof and our house had to do service as a writing base, schoolroom and pirate's hideout, often simultaneously. To Astrid, Caitriona and Christopher, my gratitude, thanks and love. (And kids, you'll be pleased that the rabbit from *Monty Python and the Holy Grail* made an appearance.)

Finally, I am grateful to Jesus, for leading, guiding and shaping my life over thirty years of following him, through good times and bad. It is my hope and my prayer that this book will point people clearly and persuasively towards him.